navigating the seven seas

Melvin G. Williams Sr. and Melvin G. Williams Jr.

navigating the seven seas

LEADERSHIP LESSONS
OF THE FIRST AFRICAN AMERICAN
FATHER AND SON TO SERVE
AT THE TOP IN THE U.S. NAVY

NAVAL INSTITUTE PRESS
Annapolis, Maryland

Naval Institute Press
291 Wood Road
Annapolis, MD 21402

Library of Congress Cataloging-in-Publication Data
Williams, Melvin G., Sr.
Navigating the seven seas : leadership lessons of the first African American father and son to serve at the top in the U.S. Navy / Melvin G. Williams Sr. and Melvin G. Williams Jr.
p. cm.
Includes bibliographical references and index.
ISBN 978-1-59114-960-6 (pbk. : alk. paper) 1. Williams, Melvin G., Sr. 2. Williams, Melvin G., Jr. 3. United States. Navy—African Americans—Biography. 4. United States. Navy—Officers—Biography. 5. Leadership—United States. I. Williams, Melvin G., Jr. II. Title.
V63.W545A3 2011
658.4'092—dc22

2010042592

Printed in the United States of America on acid-free paper

22 21 20 19 18 17 13 12 11 10 9 8

For Dora Ruth Williams and Donna Ree Williams,
our respective loving and supportive wives
of nearly ninety years combined

CONTENTS

Acknowledgments ix
Introduction xi

One **character** 1
Two **competence** 29
Three **courage** 51
Four **commitment** 71
Five **caring** 101
Six **communicating** 117
Seven **community** 139

Summary 163
Notes 167
Index 171

ACKNOWLEDGMENTS

We would like to thank Dora Ruth Williams and Donna R. Williams for their enduring support throughout our careers and lives, and for their edits of this book.

We thank Glenn Knoblock, Richard Miller, and Chester Wright for their input, and for their historical accounts of the overlooked contributions of Navy messmen and stewards.

We would also like to acknowledge several people separately. I (Melvin G. Williams Sr.) give special acknowledgment to the many who showed me how to care for others on the job, help others to succeed, and unselfishly support the mission. Friendship transcended skin color; often I was the only black sailor on the ship. I thank all the caring people with whom I worked: Boney, Richard Chidsey, James Cross, Barry Danforth, Archie Denson, Robert Haynes, Bill Holdforth, James L. Holloway III, Kimsey from Georgia, Hugh McCracken, James Mullin, Pelletier, Bill Pentell, Woody Pickren, Chuck Priest, Bob Reynolds, Jamie Rodriguez, Albert Smith, Ed Steiner, Bill Waterhouse, Roscoe Williams, Fred Umayam, Elmo Zumwalt Jr., and many others.

I (Melvin G. Williams Jr.) give special thanks to the many who helped me to develop. I observed many leaders and endeavored to follow in the path of some of these remarkable people as I navigated forward during my career. They include Chuck Beers, Skip Bowman, James Cartwright, fellow members of the U.S. Submarine Force Centennial Seven, Kirk Donald, Jerry Ellis, Malcolm Fages, Ed Giambastiani, the Golden Thirteen, Samuel Gravely, Dick Hartman, K. T. Hoephner, James L. Holloway III, Dr. Martin Luther King Jr., Jim Metzger, Mike Mullen, John Padgett, B. J. Penn, Hyman G. Rickover, Gary Roughead, Frank Stewart, Paul Sullivan, Carl Trost, USNA '78 classmates, Robert Willard, Melvin G. Williams Sr., and Elmo Zumwalt Jr.

We both indeed thank Tom Wilkerson, Tom Cutler, Rick Russell, Annie Rehill, and others at the U.S. Naval Institute for their input and superb support for this book. And, of course, we thank the U.S. Navy for providing us with the opportunity to serve and to lead.

INTRODUCTION

Navigating the Seven Seas is an account of the leadership experiences of a father and son. Writing this book was difficult for us, because we are by nature introverted and prefer to remain footnotes in Navy personnel files. We decided to go ahead because of the small chance that a few readers might consider service and leadership as a result of our story.

We are not experts in the theoretical aspects of leadership. Countless books have been written by those who have studied and adeptly analyzed the subject. These excellent works populate libraries and bookstores around the world. Our book, *Navigating the Seven Seas*, is simply an account of the experiences, opinions, and recommendations of a couple of sailors who served as leaders in the U.S. Navy.

The book is intended to be another resource to those of any age who are interested in leadership, serve as leaders, or would like to gain insight into our story.

That story is somewhat unique: in the 235-year history of the U.S. Navy, we are the first—and to date the only—African

American father and son of whom one reached the highest enlisted leadership rank of master chief, E-9, with final assignment as a command master chief, and the other the high officer leadership rank of vice admiral, O-9, with final assignment as a fleet commander. These experiences involved hard-won lessons that we believe can be useful to anyone studying the subject of leadership or trying to make best use of opportunities available toward upward mobility, while also serving others.

I (Melvin Sr.) served for twenty-seven years (1951–78); Melvin G. Williams Jr. served for thirty-two (1978–2010), nearly sixty consecutive years across two generations. As a military member committed to the Navy, I believed it to be part of my duty to offer my views on important topics such as racial discrimination. To do this effectively I had to improve my communication skills, as anyone who wishes to help improve things must strive to do. I wrote many "Dear Sir" letters to Navy leadership, a few of which are included as examples in this book.

I attained a professional milestone in 1977, when I became one of the few submarine-qualified African Americans to have the opportunity to serve as command master chief of a large surface ship. Mel Jr. reached a milestone in 1994, when he became the first African American in history to command a nuclear-powered strategic ballistic-missile submarine. In 2008 Mel Jr. became a fleet commander and the first African American to command the U.S. Second Fleet, which has its maritime headquarters at Norfolk, Virginia.

Others in our family have also volunteered to serve in the armed forces. My granddaughter Dallis Coleman is a captain in the U.S. Air Force. And on 2 July 2010, in a special ceremony conducted by video teleconference, my son promoted my grandson Ahmed Williamson to the rank of lieutenant colonel in the U.S. Marine Corps. Vice Admiral Mel Williams Jr. conducted the ceremony from Norfolk. In attendance were Ahmed's mother (my daughter Sharon); his wife, Mattrice; and their three children. Ahmed was on deployment in Iraq.

The title of our book is a nautical play on words. *Navigating* is the art and science of knowing one's location while moving safely and in a timely manner to a destination. *The Seven Seas* proposes a nautical theme representing the maritime domain of the U.S. Navy. The historical Seven Seas are the Black Sea, Caspian Sea, Persian Gulf, Red Sea, Mediterranean Sea, Adriatic Sea, and Arabian Sea, which is part of the Indian Ocean.

The experiences of a master chief and vice admiral show how we navigated to a destination of increased leadership responsibilities through our Seven Cs: character, competence, courage, commitment, caring, communicating, and community.

Although the context of our experiences is the Navy, we believe these Seven Leadership Cs are relevant to all fields, regardless of the reader's occupation or leadership situation, whether that may be military or civilian, or in public or private industry—and regardless of the reader's background, culture, and gender.

This book also tells the story of how a large organization such as the U.S. Navy can make institutional and cultural change. The Navy is a success story in that it shows how an institution can transform and demonstrate through action its stated values and principles. In our view, although the Navy still has work to do, significant progress has been made toward ensuring that all men and women of diverse backgrounds, cultures, and experience levels have the opportunity to realize their full potential. Individual worth and contributions are valued far more than they once were, and everyone is challenged to lead far more than was once the case.

This book addresses several implied questions regarding who a leader is, what a leader does, and why and how a leader performs. How did a father and son, each a black man in the U.S. Navy (minorities), each standing barely 5 feet 9 inches (not tall), and with a quiet, unassuming demeanor (not forceful), reach the opportunity to serve in top senior leadership positions?

As you read this book, we hope you will discover answers to these questions and conclude that if we could navigate to a destination of increased leadership responsibility, then you can as well. Leadership is an art and a science that can be learned, practiced, and refined. There is no stereotype or mold for leaders.

We hope you will find some useful ideas here. We certainly enjoy our service and are honored to be able to share parts of our experiences in uniform as we navigated the Seven Seas.

LEADERSHIP SEVEN Cs

Character
Integrity
Determination
Positive Attitude
Humility
Servant

Competence
Progress
Performance
Judgment
Continual Improvement

Courage
Accountability
Decisiveness
Initiative
Selflessness

Commitment
Service
Goals
Teamwork
Excellence

Caring
Self
Faith
Family
People
Leader

Communicating
Listening
Transmitting
Achieving Understanding
Inspiring

Community
Diversity
Mentoring
Assimilating
Youth

Leadership is the *art* and *science* of achieving desired effectiveness by making decisions, developing people, creating teamwork, serving needs, and inspiring action to realize the leader's vision.

It must be shaped and applied as a function of the leader, followers, and environmental conditions—with the need to adapt and adjust over time. Leadership can be learned. The Seven Cs are a helpful way to think about ways to learn and improve on this phenomenon of human behavior.

character is the most important Leadership C. It is the core of the leader, essential to the end, ways, and means of ***realizing the leader's vision.*** Leaders must have a vision of the future; they must be forward-looking and capable of regarding and anticipating the future environment, challenges, and opportunities.

A great vision statement is not leadership. Rather, it indicates great staff work and literary skill. But the formulation of the leader's vision, the team's understanding of that vision, the commitment to take right and timely action repeatedly, over time, toward the realization of the vision are central to leadership.

competence Leadership involves having competence in ***achieving desired effectiveness*** (results, performance, or outcomes), as defined by the leader. A leader must be competent as he or she guides the organization.

courage Leadership necessitates courage in ***making decisions***. Leaders should consider the facts, the opinions of a diverse group, instincts and intuition, and be decisive at the right time.

commitment A commitment to ***developing people*** is essential. The better prepared a team's individuals are for achieving the desired effectiveness, the higher the chances of success. This means providing opportunity for them to realize their full potential. The leader must be capable of trusting others, which necessitates accepting risks associated with delegating authority, and permitting some mistakes by those gaining experience. Developing people means providing for education, training, and mentoring. Developing current and future leaders is a leader's responsibility.

caring Leadership includes caring and ***serving needs.*** Individual people, money, and time are all required to accomplish an objective, and the team as a whole has different requirements. The leader must remain aware of all of these and work diligently to obtain needed resources, while also having consideration of people's needs.

communicating ***Inspiring action*** is accomplished through communicating. People want to be inspired by the leader, who provides a sense of purpose and a reason for commitment to the team's effort. However, an inspirational speech without a plan, and without the right and timely action, may prove to be labor lost. The leader needs to develop forward-looking plans with the team, and take action while creating a sense of urgency. Leaders must assess progress (that is, they must measure and see for themselves), adjust, adapt, and execute.

community Leadership involves regard for the community when ***creating teamwork.*** With individuals who are better prepared and developed, the leader must work to create a cohesive team, so that the whole group is greater than the sum of the individuals. Cooperation is vital.

One story that exemplifies the essence of our Leadership Seven Cs is the Haiti relief effort in January 2010. U.S. Navy and Marine Corps personnel rapidly responded to help.

In the late afternoon on 12 January 2010, a 7.0-level earthquake struck southern Haiti, knocking down buildings, destroying shelters, and eliminating critical sources of food, water, and electricity for the poorest nation in the Western hemisphere. The United States and the international community immediately reached out to provide aid and assistance.

As guided by the leadership of Admiral John C. Harvey Jr., Commander, U.S. Fleet Forces, the men and women who served with me (Vice Admiral Mel Williams Jr., Commander, U.S. Second Fleet) took action to ***realize my vision*** for this naval force provision effort. My vision was "to provide the best humanitarian-assistance and disaster response capability soonest," to Commander, U.S. Southern Command and Commander, U.S. Fourth Fleet.

The ***character*** of the Navy and Marine Corps leaders involved in this effort had all the elements of integrity, determination, positive attitude, humility, and servant leadership.

Today's sailors and marines are primarily America's youth who have volunteered to serve the nation. They are men and women from diverse backgrounds and cultures who share the same values: honor, courage, and commitment. On a day-to-day basis, they train for and perform in combat situations, and they also expertly help to prevent wars. When needed, they fight and win our nation's wars. And they help partner nations build their strength to provide their own security and stability. They are a global force for good.

Today's sailors and marines possess the ***competence*** to overcome adversity, accomplish any task, and ***achieve desired effectiveness***.

We saw young sailors and marines who had recently returned home from long deployments overseas, including combat operations, and many who were about to depart overseas on long deployments. They joined together as a community-strength team to help a people in need.

We witnessed the rapid choreography of steps needed to load ships with supplies, equipment, food, and water. We heard no complaints from any of our young people. Instead, we heard voices of dedicated people with a sense of urgency and compassion, who knew that their actions could save the lives of thousands of Haitians.

It took the ***courage*** of many leaders ***to make the tough decisions*** that contributed to the timely, safe, and effective relief support for the strong but truly in-need Haitian people.

As a result of the U.S. Navy and Marine Corps ***commitment*** to ***developing our people***, our sailors and marines were ready for the task. Their superb training and development translated into real-time positive action when it was required.

Although most of our ships and capabilities were about a three-day transit from the U.S. East Coast to Haiti, our sailors and marines pulled together, loaded ships, and got under way in half the time it would have taken under normal conditions (normally four days to get ready and under way).

The aircraft carrier USS *Carl Vinson* (CVN-70) arrived on station off Haiti within three and a half days after the earthquake and immediately began to provide humanitarian assistance and disaster response. Within a few more days, more than 12,000 sailors and marines from numerous ships arrived in support. This included the hospital ship USNS *Comfort* (T-AH 20).

This team of ***caring*** professions joined the U.S. Coast Guard, Army, Air Force, other U.S. government and nongovernmental organizations and agencies, other international navies, and the international community to help the government of Haiti ***serve the needs*** of their people.

As the commanders and leaders who served in Second Fleet adeptly worked toward ***communicating*** the vision for the relief effort, they in fact achieved understanding among our people, and they ***inspired action***—which ultimately led to success.

As of this writing, much remains to be done to improve conditions in this small nation. But the selfless, rapid, professional, and heartfelt response, and the ***community***-strength ***teamwork*** by the Navy–Marine Corps team, exemplified the essence of the Leadership Seven Cs.

They made all of us proud.

Leadership is the *art* and *science* of achieving desired effectiveness by making decisions, developing people, creating teamwork, serving needs, and inspiring action to realize the leader's vision.

In the following pages, the master chief insignia is used to introduce passages written by Master Chief Williams. Passages written by Admiral Williams are introduced by a row of three stars, ★★★ signifying the ranked attained by the admiral.

navigating
the seven seas

Chapter One

character

Character is the most important Leadership C. It is the core of the leader, essential to the end, ways, and means of *realizing the leader's vision*. Leaders must have a vision of the future; they must be forward-looking and capable of regarding and anticipating the future environment, challenges, and opportunities.

A great vision statement is not leadership. Rather, it indicates great staff work and literary skill. But the formulation of the leader's vision, the team's understanding of that vision, the commitment to take right and timely action repeatedly, over time, toward the realization of the vision are central to leadership.

Character is important. We believe that an individual's character—personal values in terms of doing things right, the way mistakes are handled, and individual differences that define who we are—is the foundation of leadership.

Eleanor Roosevelt said: "Somehow we learn who we really are and then live with that decision."[1]

God created each of us in his likeness; however we, as humans, are fallible. We make mistakes. Both of us have made many mistakes throughout our service as leaders in the U.S. Navy, too many to be adequately captured (or useful) in this book. Nevertheless, as we were navigating the Seven Seas, we found again and again that ***character was clearly the most important Leadership C.*** Consider its key aspects:

- **integrity**
  Consistency of actions, values, methods, measures, and principles. The quality of honesty and truthfulness regarding motivations for your actions. Trustworthiness matters.

- **determination**
  The act of coming to a decision, or of fixing or setting a purpose. Ignore obstacles and barriers. Challenge assumptions. ***Realizing the leader's vision*** takes determination. It is the leader's character that guides the ways and means of achieving the end.

- **positive attitude**
  Maintain a positive attitude despite the day-to-day challenges. This is good for your health and for organiza-

tional effectiveness. It also tends to create opportunities for the individual. Smiling is contagious. A sense of humor helps. Be optimistic.

- **humility**

  Give credit to others and the team; be silent on self, but have strong self-confidence.

- **servant leadership**

  Serve others through leadership.

The core values of honor, courage, and commitment are the principles on which the U.S. Navy and Marine Corps were founded. They continue to guide those who serve today. These core values certainly have relevance regardless of one's occupation or leadership situation, and regardless of background, culture, and gender.

HONOR

I am accountable for my professional and personal behavior. I will be mindful of the privilege I have to serve my fellow Americans. I will:

- Abide by an uncompromising code of integrity, taking full responsibility for my actions and keeping my word.
- Conduct myself in the highest ethical manner in relationships with seniors, peers, and subordinates.
- Be honest and truthful in my dealings within and outside the Department of the Navy.
- Make honest recommendations to my seniors and peers and seek honest recommendations from junior personnel.

- Encourage new ideas and deliver bad news forthrightly.
- Fulfill my legal and ethical responsibilities in my public and personal life.

[Williams SR]

FAMILY BACKGROUND

Both of my parents, Robert (1903–93) and Dimple (1909–96) Williams were born in Mississippi: Robert in Greenwood on 24 January 1903; Dimple in Corinth on 28 July 1909. My father was the youngest of John and Sylvia Williams's six children, and the only male. The Williams family generally had a fair or light-brown complexion and some Caucasian features. They were of average height. I found them reluctant to discuss family history. Skin color was a major issue within the African American community during this period, and to some extent today as well. I noted that my father and his sisters all married people of dark complexion, with the exception of Aunt Nettie, who married a light-skinned Hispanic named Bernard Acara.

My mother, whose maiden name was Dimple Mannings, was the sixth child in a family of four girls and four boys. Their parents were Lushus Mannings and Ida Dilworth. The Mannings were generally tall (except the youngest girl, the petite Aunt Flora) and slim, with dark complexions and distinctively African features. My mother stood at five feet nine inches; I barely reached her height.

I never met or shared time with any of my great-grandparents or grandparents, who were deceased. But my parents shared bits of information about them. Horace and Harriet Mannings, West and Sally Dilworth were my mother's grandparents. I do not know the names of my father's grandparents, but I do know that on both sides of the family my great-grandparents were born into slavery. The next generation, my grandparents, eventually became tenant farmers and sharecroppers. On each side they sought better lives by eventually moving from farm life in the South to the urban North.

According to Williams family folklore, my father and his sisters migrated from Mississippi following the great flood of 1927. My mother, her sisters, and one brother moved north after their father's death. Migration brought these two sides of my family to Cairo, Illinois, where they met. Eventually they both landed in East St. Louis, Illinois, where my mother and father were married. My parents had no more than fourth-grade educations, but they did as well as could be expected while enduring the country's economic depression of 1929 through the early 1930s.

I was born on 27 May 1933 in East St. Louis, the oldest of four boys and four girls. Our early life was rather difficult, as it was for so many others who grew up poor in the depression years. During my infancy, our family moved across the Mississippi River to St. Louis, Missouri's north side, where over time we established our footprint. Here I shared experiences and learned from other family members.

We lived in a racially diverse community, in a small apartment. There was one bathroom in the hallway, shared by four families. Our next-door neighbors were of Jewish background. As young kids, we made friends with the neighbors and played stickball with the remnants of broomsticks from a straw-broom factory located on the other side of our apartment building.

I remember several other factories in our neighborhood. One manufactured wooden barrels, another made light bulbs, and one company designed aircraft. There was a pickle factory and a shoe factory. Things were made in America back then.

I recall seeing the hardworking people of Polish, Italian, German, and Irish backgrounds in these factories, but I do not remember seeing any African Americans in them. Some of the few places that hired African Americans back then included the federal barge lines on the Mississippi. My father worked as a longshoreman, loading and unloading barges. This was considered a good job for a black man. Additionally, a few blacks were lucky enough to find work in the steel mill in East St. Louis, in the slaughterhouses at the meat-packing plants, at the Monsanto chemical company as janitors, and as waiters, dishwashers, and cooks at the St. Louis country club.

My mother was what was termed a domestic house worker, meaning she cleaned other people's houses.

By 1946, many of the factories closed and the economic base dried up. The community slowed down as most of the various ethnicities left, except blacks and Italians. This was our home.

My wife, Ruth, whose parents were Robert and Ella (Graves) Pettes, was the youngest of fifteen children. The Pettes were from Las Cruces, New Mexico, via Oklahoma and Texas. In 1922 they moved to New Mexico under the duress of racist pressures and physical threats to their well-being. They were initially reluctant to discuss family history, but we later discovered that Robert and Ella were both half African American and half Native American. In those years, especially in New Mexico, Native Americans were sent to reservation camps. So they found that whether Native American or African American, in our country during the 1920s, one had to keep quiet about background and endeavor to find a place to live in peace.

Today, when Ruth and I share time with our current generations, we make it a point to discuss family background. We are now great-grandparents who have had the opportunity to help shape the lives of each new generation. We think it is important for our youth to know how far we have come as a people, and also that continued performance and effort will be needed in the future for them to realize their full potential in our great nation.

EDUCATION

I praise my parents for having the courage to endure adversity and inspire each of their children to pursue an education as a means for personal growth. This ***courage*** and ***emphasis on education*** were also perhaps something that our children—Sharon, Veronica, Mel Jr., and Kenneth—obtained from Ruth and me. To set an example, we both earned college associates' degrees when we were over forty years old.

When I was a child, each morning at the Dessalines Grammar School we recited the Pledge of Allegiance, sang the National Anthem, and then sang what has become the African American Anthem ("Lift Every Voice and Sing"). My cousin, Maurice Quarre les (about nine months older), became my best friend. We attended Dessalines together. The school was a bedrock in the community, a respected institution of learning in our diverse neighborhood.

All my grammar-school teachers were female. As I reflect back on their performance as educators and sources of influence, they were outstanding.

I remember taking an IQ test in the eighth grade and scoring quite well. This eventually resulted in my placement into an academic track in a technical high school. The school was not particularly challenging, and my grades were high without much effort.

However, in my sophomore year my mind opened to the value of learning. When I was fifteen, I had the opportunity to participate in the academic fast track at Lincoln High School in Tacoma,

Washington. My Aunt Flora and her husband, Lawrence Norman, had moved there and invited me to come to the Pacific Northwest to attend a racially integrated high school in 1948. This was a top-quality education. The teachers, facilities, and learning methods were challenging and superb. ***I was required to study and work beyond my natural ability.***

The program included typing, public speaking, and algebra. In 1948 none of these were available in the segregated schools of St. Louis, Missouri. As I graduated from high school in 1951, the Korean War had recently begun. Many classmates and I elected to serve in the military. I enlisted in the U.S. Navy in 1951.

MILITARY BEGINNINGS—AND CONCLUSIONS

I went to boot camp at San Diego, California, as the only African American in my company. Afterward I was assigned as a steward. I did not realize until I assembled with the others who had been selected as stewards that we were all African American. Boot camp was integrated, but the post–boot camp stewards group was segregated. We were all high school graduates and dismayed by the process. As I entered the fleet, I met my fellow stewards who, despite their directed career field, maintained positive and professional attitudes.

I recall my first off-duty liberty period in San Diego during boot camp. I had decided to spend the night at a hotel in town but was denied accommodations. This was disappointing, as California had been hailed as a racially integrated state. I was further displeased to discover that some in the city were encouraging African American sailors to stay in an area about four blocks wide during our off-duty liberty time.

So it was in our segregated area of town, and in our segregated living spaces on the Navy base and ships, that we junior sailors

In 1952 Steward Apprentice (E-2) Melvin G. Williams Sr. was a student at Steward's Class A school. He graduated as the "honor man," at the top of his class. (U.S. Navy)

bonded with the more senior, mature African American petty officers. From them we learned to remain positive no matter what. They took care of us and educated us quickly on the methods and skills necessary for our survival.

They taught us that the Navy was a worthwhile venture, and that we should give it our best efforts. Considering our situation and the overall environment in 1951, I believe our mentors were successful. Of a group of about sixty, at least twelve of us eventually reenlisted and became career sailors and leaders. Those senior African American petty officers remain among my heroes to this day.

Twenty-seven years later, in June 1978, I attended Mel Jr.'s graduation from the U.S. Naval Academy. He attended my retirement from the Navy that same year, as well as my graduation from Northern Virginia Community College. Mel Jr., in my view, had always been a keen observer of life around him. He took full advantage of the opportunities afforded to him in the 1970s in our nation, and he has done quite well.

KEY INFLUENCERS OF MY CHARACTER

My ***family***, in particular my parents, set the course for me by showing through their example how to succeed. Without much education or financial means, they raised our family of ten through love, hard work, and determination.

My third-grade ***teacher***, Mrs. Pearl Moore, encouraged me to enjoy reading. She believed that I would someday do well.

My Aunt Flora was ever the adventurer and courageous about trying new things. When she and her husband invited me to Tacoma, it was a turning point in my ***education*** and outlook on opportunity.

My father-in-law, Robert A. Pettes, was truly a remarkable person who influenced me. With no formal education, he and his wife raised fifteen children as farmers in Oklahoma, Texas, and New

Mexico. As a man of ***faith, kindness, and tenacious determination***, in the 1960s he established a successful family business, Mesa Development, which is still going today. Mesa provides a clean water supply to customers in Las Cruces, New Mexico.

As I entered the U.S. Navy, my ***first chief petty officer***, Senior Chief Henry Hyman, set the right example in the areas of integrity and leadership. Later in my career my ***commanding officer*** on board the submarine USS *Thomas Jefferson* (SSBN-618, Gold crew), Captain Charles Priest, was a leadership role model. He was the best commanding officer with whom I served. I would have followed him anywhere. He was truly a highly effective leader, with humility and a sincere caring for the crew.

Admiral Elmo Zumwalt Jr. was a key influencer. In my opinion, he was the finest person ever to serve in our Navy. He led needed reforms during the early 1970s and was a champion for sailors and families. Admiral Zumwalt was the first Navy senior leader to drive equal opportunity for all people who served, including changes that raised the level of opportunity for minorities and women to equal that of others. His legacy of service and leadership lives on today. It was my privilege to serve and support him.

It was also a privilege to be influenced by Admiral Zumwalt's successor, Chief of Naval Operations ***Admiral James L. Holloway III*** (whom I served and supported in the Pentagon, 1974–76, and who spoke at Mel Jr.'s submarine change-of-command ceremony in 1997), as well as by Secretary of the Navy ***John W. Warner***, whom I served and supported in the Pentagon in 1973, and who in 1995, as a U.S. senator, visited Mel Jr.'s submarine command.

Mel Jr. and his nephew (Sharon's son) ***Ahmed Williamson*** have made us all very proud. Mel Jr. served and led his people with distinction throughout his Navy career. Ahmed, U.S. Naval Academy Class of 1994, continues to lead as a U.S. Marine Corps officer.

A lieutenant colonel, he has served two tours of duty in Iraq, one tour in Okinawa, and at Special Operations Command on his third assignment in Iraq. He is doing quite well as a leader. Mel Jr. and Ahmed both influence my retirement activities, as does my granddaughter ***Dallis (Rawls) Coleman***, Veronica's daughter, who serves as a captain in the U.S. Air Force.

My wife, ***Ruth Williams***, has stood with me over the years and remains a key influencer of my character.

INTEGRITY, DETERMINATION, POSITIVE ATTITUDE, HUMILITY, SERVANT LEADER

When I look at the future, it's so bright, it burns my eyes.
—Oprah Winfrey

Most leaders state that they emphasize the importance of ***integrity*** and honesty. Those who have actually lived by these standards have been the most successful. For me, the most meaningful repeated positive feedback I have received in this regard has been statements like: "If Mel says that he is going to do it, then you can count on it happening." This type of response has inspired me to continue maintaining integrity.

As a young sailor in the 1950s, I discovered that the steward's rating had limited opportunity for advancement for those who served within it—primarily minorities. It was difficult to watch sailors in other ratings come into the Navy after me but advance first. For eight years I remained at the third-class petty officer rank, even though my advancement test scores were always near the top.

Nevertheless, I maintained a ***positive attitude*** and was ***determined*** to advance. After eleven years in the Navy, I was advanced to second-class petty officer. I continued to work on my skills and performance, while also studying the required materials for further advancement. I quietly ordered additional course materials and studied with my shipmates.

I refused to let my early disappointments stop me from moving forward. By my twenty-fifth year of service, I was advanced to master chief petty officer. I certainly remained ***humble***, having remained in the lower ranks for so long. As I advanced, this humility and its associated empathy made me better appreciate and respect people who serve in lower positions.

I truly believe that ***leaders should serve*** their people as they lead them. This has been the case for me, both in the Navy and during my post-Navy civilian career.

[Williams JR]

FAMILY BACKGROUND

I arrived on this Earth in November 1955, about one month before Rosa Parks refused to give up her seat on a bus in Montgomery, Alabama. As an African American male who grew up in the United States when equal opportunity for all people was beginning, I felt a personal imperative to have the integrity and determination to fulfill the ***obligation*** that I truly believed I had to realize the dreams of those courageous African Americans who had come before me. I was not alone in this belief, which many African Americans in my generation shared.

My father and his parents, Dimple and Robert Williams, were hardworking individuals of solid character. My mother, Dora Ruth Williams, and her parents, Ella and Robert Pettes, were also gifted with traits including integrity, determination, a positive attitude, fairness, a personable disposition, humility, and the elements of servant leadership.

Both sides of our ***family*** were key in influencing the formation of my character. Within our immediate family, older sisters Sharon and Veronica, as well as younger brother Kenneth (diagnosed with autism), in a kind way helped me to remain humble. Thank goodness for my siblings!

Donna, my wife of more than thirty years and high school girlfriend, certainly has been a key influencer of my character. She is the most honest person I have ever known.

EARLY EDUCATION

In 1959, four years after I was born in San Diego, California, our family moved to New Orleans for my father's new Navy assignment. The following year, I began kindergarten in a segregated school. As part of my early education, I vaguely remember kids from other schools chanting, "Two, four, six, eight, we don't want to integrate!" I did not know what that meant, I just remember the chant.

From late in 1960 until about 1962, we lived in Portsmouth, Virginia, then later Norfolk. Those schools also were segregated. I do remember that my second-grade ***teacher*** took a special interest in me. I did well and learned.

From 1963 to 1968 we lived in Groton, Connecticut, where a Navy submarine base is located. This was my first opportunity to attend ***integrated schools***. The academics were challenging, the teachers caring and dedicated. I believe the very good schools in Connecticut were the foundation of my education. The fact that they were integrated helped shape my ability to blend with people of different backgrounds.

We moved to the Washington, D.C., area in 1968. I absorbed the pivotal events of that year with the eyes and mind of a thirteen-year-old: the Vietnam war, Tet Offensive, assassinations of Dr.

Martin Luther King and Robert Kennedy, racial riots, Mexico City Olympics . . . I see today that it was all part of my education. The D.C. area provided quite a vantage point from which to witness the cultural and social revolution then taking place.

EARLY WORK

As our family moved from place to place due to my father's Navy assignments, ***education*** was their number-one priority for us. Number two was participation in sports (baseball, football, basketball, and more) and other ***teamwork activities*** such as Cub Scouts and Boy Scouts for me, Girl Scouts and Awana for my sisters. My parents also allowed me to ***work*** part-time jobs, which I believe influenced my character.

During the summer months while growing up, I assisted the neighborhood garbage collector and earned a few dollars each time. I cut lawns, and in winters shoveled snow in neighborhood driveways and sidewalks for modest pay. When we moved to Temple Hills, Maryland, just outside of southeast Washington, D.C., I got a job delivering the *Washington Post* newspaper.

My father later assisted me in obtaining a job as a busboy at the Washington Navy Yard officers' club. And the wonderful job I held during high school was as a janitor in the office spaces in Iverson Mall, about two miles from our family home.

While working these jobs, I met quality, hardworking people of strong character. In retrospect, my early work was not about the money, it was about the human-to-human ***relationships*** experienced, ***discipline***, and ***character development.***

Along with the strong values of my family, my early work influenced me to desire to serve others and lead.

U.S. NAVAL ACADEMY

As a young person in a generation that believed it was our obligation to seize opportunities afforded by the Civil Rights movement, there was no question that the pursuit of higher education was in the plan. As a result of years of exposure to the Navy via my father and his friends, and a sense that one should serve others in some capacity, I sought entry to the U.S. Naval Academy in Annapolis, Maryland. I believed this path would be a good way to serve our country, become a leader of people, and earn a college degree—particularly as our family income could not afford top civilian educational institutions. The Naval Academy has no tuition, just an obligation to learn, grow, and serve as leaders in the Navy or Marine Corps after graduation.

But when I was *not* initially accepted, this helped build my character. My grades and teamwork activities in high school were good, but my Scholastic Aptitude Test scores were relatively low. In 1972, one year before my graduation from Suitland High School near Washington, D.C., I took the SATs with no practice or preparation, and performed poorly. This was a lesson learned. My character began to develop more in the area of ***determination.***

My father, who at the time was a senior chief petty officer (later a master chief), served in the Pentagon for the Secretary of the Navy and Chief of Naval Operations at the flag mess. He communicated my situation to others and learned about another option: the U.S. Naval Academy Preparatory School (NAPS).

Determined to prevail, and with the assistance of my father and the informed Pentagon leaders, I applied and was accepted to NAPS, then located in Bainbridge, Maryland (today in Newport,

Rhode Island). My father and I traveled to Baltimore, and in June 1973 I enlisted as a seaman recruit, U.S. Navy Reserves, in advance of entry to NAPS.

Shortly after my arrival at NAPS boot camp that August, each of my parents wrote me a letter of encouragement addressed to "Butch"—the childhood nickname that I have been trying, to no avail, to leave behind.

"Dear Butch," Dad wrote, "How is it going? Rough? Well hang in there and give yourself a chance to see if you like it. We have a little time to evaluate the situation to see if it is worth it to you." He got straight to the point, while at the same time demonstrating unwavering confidence in my capabilities.

This letter shows how my father taught me many of the same principles we are striving to pass on in this book. A patient and thorough guide, he pointed me toward an awareness of the opportunities that lay in front of me. He hoped I would take advantage of them, but never lost sight of the fact that ultimately I would have to find my own way in the world.

Dad never strong-armed me, never presented his views as the best way to proceed. He simply tried to help me benefit from what he had learned firsthand, while realizing that his experiences could never apply to me in exactly the same way. "If along the way you should decide to go another direction," he wrote, "don't feel that you will be letting me down. Whatever way you want to go I will support your decision." He went on:

> The only thing that I do say is learn to do something. Develop a skill or get education to learn to live by your brain. I know that this is a heavy personal sacrifice, but it is for your future. If you have feelings about going another way at the end of this year you can make your decision. You can either go ahead,

> drop out and go back to school, stay in the reserve for the other year and save your money, or go any other direction. Whatever it is you decide, be positive and serious about success and competition. Be positive. Be bold. Be determined.

My mother's letter showed the same confidence—tinged with natural maternal resistance to an offspring actually leaving the nest.

> I am beginning to have second thoughts about the school. I guess because we miss you and partly because you seemed a little sad about leaving, but I guess that is a normal reaction. But if that is your desire of endeavor, I can only feel proud and wish you all the success in the world, because things worthwhile having or accomplishing do not come easy. I believe that you have what it takes to fulfill your highest aspiration. . . . We as your parents will love you at any rate.[2]

My year at NAPS did help me to raise my SAT scores. After serving as an enlisted sailor (E-1 and E-2) for one year, I graduated from NAPS and was accepted at the U.S. Naval Academy in 1974. I was a member of the Class of 1978. For me, failure was not an option.

The mission of the U.S. Naval Academy is "to develop Midshipmen morally, mentally, and physically and to imbue them with the highest ideals of duty, honor, and loyalty in order to graduate leaders who are dedicated to a career of Naval service and have potential for future development in mind and character to assume the highest responsibilities of command, citizenship, and government."[3]

My character was certainly shaped by my experiences at the ***U.S. Naval Academy.*** The values of ***honor*** and ***integrity*** were

Mathematics major Melvin G. Williams Jr. graduated from the United States Naval Academy in 1978, in the top third of his class. (U.S. Naval Academy)

Senior Chief Petty Officer Williams was assigned as head of the Secretary of the Navy and Chief of Naval Operations flag mess in 1974, when he and Midshipman Fourth Class Williams attended the Army-Navy football game together in Philadelphia (the game's traditional location). (Courtesy of the authors)

emphasized from day one and throughout the four years. As I was challenged in the academic, military, and athletic areas, my determination to succeed grew stronger. Although my start was delayed by attending NAPS before admission, eventually I was able to reach my personal goals at the Naval Academy: superintendent's list (academics), commandant's list (military), and a varsity letter (athletics). I received a lot of ***help from classmates and instructors*** along the way.

My company officer (lieutenant commander, U.S. Navy) noted upon completion of my junior year that "Midshipman Williams, although quiet, seems to have potential." He provided me with my first opportunity to serve and to lead.

I was assigned as a company commander during summer 1977 training for the incoming class of midshipmen, the Class of 1981. This opportunity was a ***character builder***. As a result of our superb teamwork, we were selected as the color company, or highest-performing. I remain appreciative that my company officer challenged me in a leadership capacity.

I graduated from the Naval Academy in June 1978, along with 987 friends and classmates. We had experienced many high points and some lows, but the four years at this fine institution were instrumental in the development of my character.

THE RICKOVER EFFECT

Several books have been written about Admiral Hyman G. Rickover, father of the U.S. Navy's Nuclear Propulsion Program. Among them is Theodore Rockwell's *The Rickover Effect: How One Man Made a Difference* (Naval Institute Press, 1992).

In 1949 Rickover received an assignment to the Division of Reactor Development, Atomic Energy Commission, which was the

U.S. government's national effort. Later he concurrently became director of the Naval Reactors Branch in the Bureau of Ships, representing the U.S. Navy's effort. By 1954, Rickover had spearheaded the development of the world's first nuclear-powered ship, the submarine USS *Nautilus* (SSN-571). Employing a nuclear reactor, and its associated new technologies, as an energy source for ships was a transformational event in history.

Admiral Rickover's leadership, determination, technical inventiveness, and political savvy created an organization that is still admired today as one of the best in the U.S. government. In the many areas he touched, he left a legacy of excellence known as the Rickover Effect.

During my junior year at the Naval Academy, I considered service in the submarine force as my career field after graduation. My father had served in submarines, as a non-nuclear-trained enlisted man fully qualified in all other demanding aspects of these ships. So I was familiar with the exciting and challenging aspects of this force. For me to be accepted as a nuclear-trained officer in submarines, like all candidates I would have to volunteer and be personally interviewed by the head of the U.S. Navy Nuclear Propulsion Program, Admiral Rickover. This process continues today with the current head of the program.

Admiral Rickover's interviews were infamous and no doubt left each candidate with a Rickover Effect. I was no different. My interview was short. Before he abruptly asked me to leave his office, he required that I improve my academic class standing during my final Naval Academy year, that I study thirty hours per week, and that I write him a personal letter each month to inform him that I had studied the requisite hours. I was accepted into the program.

So, using the manual typewriter of the times, until I graduated in June 1978, every month I typed and forwarded this memo:

In 1977, Chief of Naval Operations Admiral James L. Holloway III (center) greeted Williams (third from left) and his family, with their friend Hospital Corpsman First Class Forest Rawls Jr. (left). Midshipman Second Class Williams stands second from left; his mother and two sisters to the right: Ruth, Sharon, and Veronica. The occasion was Master Chief Williams's departure ceremony before his transfer from the Pentagon to duty on board the USS *Piedmont* (AD-17). (U.S. Navy)

Master Chief Williams administered the oath of office to Ensign Williams shortly after his graduation and commissioning at the U.S. Naval Academy, 7 June 1978. Immediately following the oath, Master Chief Williams saluted Ensign Williams, who returned the salute and then presented a silver dollar to his father—the traditional award from a new officer who receives the first salute from an enlisted. Later that same year, Ensign Williams attended Master Chief Williams's retirement ceremony. (U.S. Navy)

From: Midshipman Melvin G. Williams, Jr.

To: Admiral Hyman G. Rickover

Subject: Study hours

I have studied 30 hours per week this month.

Very Respectfully,

MIDN M.G. Williams, Jr.

I complied with each of his requirements. My ***character development*** and experience in the program (the ***Rickover Effect***) and in submarines impressed upon me that:

- ***Integrity*** must be uncompromising. There is no such thing as part-time integrity.
- ***Responsibility*** is a condition attributable to the individual. There is no pointing a finger at others if you are responsible. Take responsibility for situations involving self, and leadership responsibility for your people and your organizational effectiveness.
- ***Excellence*** must be the standard of performance.

COMMAND

Many leaders agree that there is no greater leadership privilege than to be in command of a military unit, nor is there a greater responsibility for the success or failure of the unit than that held by the commander. Leadership effectiveness is key within any organization, whether civilian private industry, public industry, or others.

The U.S. Navy has afforded me with opportunities to command: to serve and to lead people. I am eternally grateful for these opportunities, as they have made me a better person. Command tours repeatedly reaffirmed that character is the most important leadership trait. ***Leaders must set the example.***

INTEGRITY

Maintaining integrity is instrumental in gaining the trust and confidence of your people. Whether the news is bad or good, honesty in words and deeds is the right approach. ***Trustworthiness matters.***

For me, taking a stand on universal truths or principles was a better approach than perhaps a more popular approach. ***Integrity involves reason and choice.***

The reasoning and ultimate choices made during my command were sometimes embarrassing, both for me and for the command. Nevertheless, in my view ***maintaining integrity*** helps individuals maintain peace of mind and helps organizations to achieve desired effectiveness and ***realize the leader's vision***.

DETERMINATION

During my four command assignments, there were many times when critics, obstacles, and adverse conditions conspired to render some necessary goals, objectives, or tasks too hard. My father and I happen to possess a quiet yet tenacious determination to realize our vision, and to succeed if the goals, objectives, and tasks are the right things to do.

So we ***challenged assumptions, solicited help*** from our people and senior leaders, and ***pressed forward***. The people within our commands were able to perform well despite critics, obstacles, and adverse conditions.

POSITIVE ATTITUDE

It has been my experience that leaders tend to receive a fair share of ***bad news on a regular basis***. I observed my father and his friends, who were bountiful in intelligence and talent but initially limited in opportunity. Yet they still maintained a positive attitude in the conduct of duties and in their general disposition in life.

So as I grew, developed, and served in command and beyond, I made the ***choice to maintain a positive attitude***, despite challenges and bad news. Being cheerful—and exhibiting an occasional smile and a sense of humor—helps.

Relationships are an important aspect of being human. People tend to want to associate with positive people. And, in my experience, people with positive attitudes also tend to be the ***recipients of additional opportunities***. In command, when the leader is positive despite challenges and bad news, this provides strength and hope to others who are in the leader-follower relationship.

As Norman Vincent Peale said, "Any fact facing us is not as important as our attitude toward it, for that determines our success or failure."[4] I believe attitude is essentially a ***repository of our thoughts and beliefs***. My choice is to try to maintain a positive attitude. One of my favorite sayings is:

> Be careful of your thoughts, for your thoughts become words.
> Be careful of your words, for your words become actions.
> Be careful of your actions, for your actions become habits.
> Be careful of your habits, for your habits become your character.
> Be careful of your character, for your character becomes your destiny.[5]

HUMILITY

It is natural for a leader to accept responsibility when things go wrong, and to give credit to the individuals and collective team when they go well. But truth be said, when the TV camera crew is gone and the bright lights turned off, does the leader really mean it? My father and I mean it. Possibly our introverted personalities play a role.

SERVANT LEADERS

My passion is "service to others through leadership," along lines defined by Robert Greenleaf.

In 1977 Robert Greenleaf coined the term "servant leadership," which he described as follows:

> It begins with the natural feeling that one wants to serve, to serve first. Then conscious choice brings one to aspire to lead. . . . The leader-first and servant-first are two extreme types. . . . The difference manifests itself in the care taken by the servant-first to make sure that the other people's highest priority needs are being served. The best test, and difficult to administer, is: Do those served grow as persons, do they grow while being served, become healthier, wiser, freer, more autonomous, more likely to become servants? And what is the effect on the least privileged in society? Will they benefit or at least not be further deprived?[6]

Chapter Two

competence

> Leadership involves having competence in *achieving desired effectiveness* (results, performance, or outcomes) as defined by the leader. A leader must be competent as he or she guides the organization.

Effective leaders must know their job. They must get the job done, repeatedly, while continually improving as conditions change over time. Henry David Thoreau said: "If one advances confidently in the direction of his dreams, and endeavors to live the life which he has imagined, he will meet with a success unexpected in common hours."[7]

Competence is important. It is essential for a leader to have credibility and to gain trust and confidence. We believe that to "advance confidently," one must be competent.

And we believe that a leader's competence is an essential element of the real organizational effectiveness, versus the perceived reputation of the leader and her or his organization. The leader's competence is essential to ***achieving desired effectiveness.***

Thus, ***competence*** was the ***second Leadership C*** as we navigated. Its key aspects include:

- **progress**
  Make progress via preparedness (education, training, practice to gain experience) combined with opportunity (seek and seize leadership opportunities to serve others). Get help, heed the wisdom of experience. Seek mentorship. Ask those who have been there before. Listen and learn.
- **performance**
  Get the job done right. Have a vision of the future, while achieving individual and organizational ***desired effectiveness.***
- **judgment**
  Develop sound judgment by continually increasing knowledge and experience over time. This is critical to effective decision making.
- **continual improvement**
  Assume that change is a constant, and the status quo a short-duration concept. That said, organizations and individuals will always change, either toward improvement or for the worse, based on relative changes in the local organizational or global environment.

Thus, as a leader you should pursue change toward continual or gradual improvement. Maintaining the status quo for a long time will no doubt result in competitors getting ahead of you and your organization. Long-duration status-quo performance will result in regression, as the world around you improves. Seek personal and professional growth. Learn, read, and experience new things.

[Williams SR]

PROGRESS

As I served in the Navy, I always worked hard to prepare myself for advancement and ***progression*** up the ranks so that I had more responsibility to serve more sailors. I ***prepared*** myself.

Back in high school, I had been able to develop as a leader through several opportunities. As a fairly good athlete, my best sport was track and field, specializing in the sprint events. I also made the starting team in baseball and was elected captain of the football team. Sports provided me with ***leadership opportunities*** in high school, and later in the Navy as well.

Despite the fact that during my Navy assignments I was usually the only black person and a steward in the 1950s, I took the opportunity to play sports on the command teams. I was elected captain of the command's softball team on board three different ships.

In 1963 on the *Thomas Jefferson*, a nuclear-powered strategic ballistic-missile submarine, the captain authorized a ship's newspaper. I took the opportunity to write an article in response to the annual Fourth of July message that the fleet commander had promulgated. "Although July 4th has passed by calendar date," I wrote, "we, with serious thought and a real look at our history, must realize that every day is July 4th in spirit and purpose." I reflected on previous generations' sacrifices in defense of freedom, and reminded readers "of the sacrifices that must be made by us in this generation, in order that we may have something of value to pass on to those that follow."[8]

The day after this was published, I was asked to serve as an editor for the newspaper. This was quite an honor for one of the few blacks on board the submarine, as well as for a steward. I took that opportunity and continued to grow and learn. My July 4th article also impressed our commanding officer, who decided to forward it to the fleet commander. His favorable response was later included in our newspaper.

My submarine service was filled with other opportunities. On board the *Jefferson*, the executive officer assigned me as the battle-stations phone talker in the sub's control room. This was a critical communications position during the ship's most operationally active periods.

Later, as a first-class petty officer, I was given the opportunity to qualify as chief of the watch, a key position on a submarine as it operates safely at sea. Imagine a blindfolded police officer safely and effectively directing rush-hour traffic in New York's Times Square. The blindfold is analogous to the lack of windows in a submarine, meaning one cannot actually see potential hazards in the surrounding operating environment. It is a busy position.

I prepared myself and qualified. Qualification is an extensive and demanding process, in which one must thoroughly understand all relevant systems and procedures—academically and through practical performance.

In 1967, Steward First Class Williams (center front) was determined to retain a positive attitude regardless of the problems, often racially motivated, with which he and his family had to contend. Emphasizing education, to lead by example both he and Ruth (left) later earned college associate's degrees. Sharon, Melvin Jr., and Veronica stand behind their parents; next to his father sits Kenneth. (Courtesy of the authors)

The *Thomas Jefferson* (SSBN-618) under way on the surface, full speed, during one of her sea trials. Steward Second Class Williams boarded her in 1963 and later became an editor for the ship's newspaper, the *Snorkel*. (U.S. Navy)

A few years later I was transferred to another submarine, the USS *James K. Polk* (SSBN-645). A friend of mine was already assigned to the *Polk* as I arrived. He had evidently informed the newspaper staff that I had written articles and edited the *Jefferson*'s newspaper. Accordingly, before I even knew the names of the *Polk*'s crew members, I was approached and asked to serve as an editor for the newspaper.

Serving as a steward, I did my best. It was a surprise to me in 1968 when I was selected to serve on the presidential yacht *Sequoia*. I was honored to serve Presidents Lyndon Johnson and Richard Nixon.

Opportunities continued, as I was later selected to serve as leading chief for the Secretary of the Navy and Chief of Naval Operations flag mess at the Pentagon. Secretaries of the Navy included the Honorables Paul Ignatius, John Chafee, John Warner (later senator, and in 1995 a visitor on board Mel Jr.'s submarine USS *Nebraska* [SSBN-739]), and J. William Middendorf II. Chiefs of Naval Operations included Admirals Thomas Moorer, Elmo Zumwalt Jr., and James L. Holloway III, who commissioned Mel Jr. as a naval officer at the U.S. Naval Academy graduation in 1978, and who in 1997 spoke at his change-of-command ceremony on the *Nebraska*.

The final opportunity of significance for me in the Navy was my last assignment as command master chief on board the destroyer tender USS *Piedmont* (AD-17). It was a true honor when my commanding officer, Captain Lyle Armel, selected me for this position. The command master chief is the key leadership link between the commanding officer, officers, and crew. My guess is that the captain selected me because he may have believed I was the leader best prepared to deal with the issues and challenges that the ship and crew were attempting to address. In 1977, many of these were related to

On board the *Thomas Jefferson*, Steward Second Class Williams (opposite, above, and right) learned from the ship's commanding officer, Captain Charles Priest, valuable lessons about how to lead effectively. (Courtesy of the authors)

addiction. Again I did my best, as discussed further in the following section ("Performance"). In all it was a rewarding experience.

During the 1970s in our country, illegal drug use and racial issues emerged concurrently with unrest associated with the conduct of an unpopular war in Vietnam. These issues carried over into the military. As command master chief, I accepted responsibility for our sailors who needed guidance to conform to Navy core values, and for their not replicating the negative conduct that was then being exhibited elsewhere in society.

I was determined to make a positive difference. For example, in an attempt to discourage smoking marijuana on the ship's open deck at night, we implemented a system we called COW POW, in which the chief of the watch was teamed with a petty officer of the watch. Each night the more senior COW and a junior POW moved about and patrolled the decks, including small spaces and cubbyholes. I do not have concrete data regarding the effectiveness of this effort. But we did see that senior individuals were able to influence, in a positive way, junior petty officers as they walked about the ship.

From what I can observe in today's Navy, there is no tolerance for illegal drug use. To be sure, there may be occasional problems out there, but I do feel that the issues are continually being evaluated, and that today's Navy leadership is applying its best efforts.

PERFORMANCE

The bottom line is that we must perform to the best of our ability in the jobs that we have. ***Performance is key.***

After reporting on board the *Piedmont* in late 1976, I saw the many issues and challenges with which the ship and crew were struggling. There was a culture of drug use, morale was low, and conduct problems were linked to racial attitudes. Captain Armel and I worked together to turn things around. We performed in a way that involved every person on the ship.

We eliminated the drug problem—which, through leaders' concerted efforts Navy-wide, was essentially eliminated by the late 1980s. We addressed racial attitudes by implementing several programs that required crew members to better understand one another. In regular meetings of racially integrated groups of sailors, perceptions and issues were discussed until awareness improved. We changed day-to-day policies on the ship, with the goal of ensuring that each individual had equal opportunity to enjoy the comforts of off-duty time, and equal opportunity to pursue professional development during on-duty time.

Another positive morale factor was our improvement of food service on the ship. It was my responsibility to ensure that good-quality meals were prepared and served in all the mess halls: the crew's, first-class petty officers', chief petty officers', and officers' wardroom. I worked with our team to develop an improved plan for food service and menus. We submitted the plan to the captain, who said to proceed. Toward building consistency in our standards and quality of service, we instituted an exchange program whereby food-service workers were rotated between the various mess halls. This worked well.

The crew generally elected to segregate by race and ethnicity in the mess areas. We had some complaints from black sailors about the perceived lower quality of their spaces. The seats were more run down, they said, and the tables not as nice as those in the white sailors' areas. Some sailors from racial and ethnic minority groups complained that their preferred foods were not included on the menus. Black sailors periodically wanted soul food, while Filipinos and other minorities wanted their foods, similar to what they had enjoyed in the company of their family members.

So we established a menu-review board whose members were the customers. All pay grades, races and ethnicities, and the most vocal members were represented. I informed the board that they now owned the results, whether good or bad. We ensured that good nutritional guidelines were followed and set up two mess lines. One was for hamburgers, pizza, fried chicken wings, French fries, and so on; the other for more wholesome foods. It all worked out, as indicated by the fact that when the *Piedmont* was in port, there were no more pizza-delivery orders from in town.

Within a month, we had a supply inspection by a team of experts from the naval-district headquarters. After three days the leaders announced their results in the wardroom. Captain Armel was informed that his storekeepers and ship servicemen had *not* done well—but there was also good news: his food-service personnel had performed very well. They were to be nominated for the Food Service Ney Award, an annual recognition of the best in food services for each of the different-size ships.

The captain had initially appeared distressed, but this announcement brought tears of joy to his eyes. We gave credit to the menu-review board. Throughout the ship there was a great sense of pride. Even though we did not win the Ney Award that year, the inspection team told us they were going to incorporate our system as a guide for future inspections.

From a leadership standpoint, this final assignment was a success based on the true application of each of the Leadership Seven Cs.

JUDGMENT AND CONTINUAL IMPROVEMENT

By the time I became a senior chief petty officer in the Navy, I had developed a fairly good sense of ***judgment*** based on the ***knowledge*** and ***experience*** I had acquired over twenty-plus years of service. I also strongly believed that the U.S. Navy needed to ***improve*** in providing opportunity for all people.

I loved the Navy. Accordingly, I quietly pressed senior leaders toward action that would improve conditions for all people who served. This method did achieve measurable results, as the author of *Black Men and Blue Water*, Chester A. Wright, recently documented. Writing from the perspective of the 1970s, he noted:

> Today the Navy's two top stewards, for that is what they always will be though wearing the new designation "Mess Management Specialist," [are] probably two of the best and brightest Master Chiefs in the Service. The top steward in the Supply Corps is George A. Cohen, a skillful administrator and teacher. Cohen recognized and upgraded the cooks' and stewards' school at San Diego, and is now assisting the Bureau [of Personnel] with the mess specialist rating.
>
> Master Chief Melvin Williams, the top steward in the Navy, administers the Secretary of the Navy and the Chief of Naval Operations mess in the Pentagon. Williams served four Secretaries of the Navy. Williams is not a mere administrator but a teacher and diplomat as well. It is upon these two men that the Bureau of Personnel, Supply and the CNO [Admiral Zumwalt] have relied for advice in conducting the amalgamation of the two branches of service in an equitable manner. The Navy and the stewards are indeed lucky to have the dedication and keen analytical minds of these two men. Both are dedicated and possess vast knowledge, resources, insight and experience oriented to bring to the problem of amalgamation.[9]

★★★

[Williams JR]

- Competence is essential. Leaders must have it for self-confidence and credibility, and to inspire trust and confidence among their followers.
- Effective leaders must know their job.
- Effective leaders must get the job done, repeatedly, while continually improving as conditions change over time.

PROGRESS

Many people early in their development demonstrate high intellects. When tested, they have exceptionally high IQs. Some of them are even "scary smart"—those who complete tests early, before the allotted time has expired. They obtain perfect scores and then seek ways to obtain extra credit (better than perfect?). I am not one of those people.

With this admission, I also share my observation that each of us has a natural ability. Many factors contribute to the level and extent of that natural ability. For me, in high school I could effortlessly maintain high grades while participating in sports, dating, and working part-time.

But the SATs were a wakeup call. The U.S. Naval Academy was beyond my natural ability. The Navy Nuclear Propulsion Program was well beyond my natural ability. In order to succeed, I had to learn how to study effectively. I had to seek help from instructors and classmates. The point is that ***to be competent when challenged beyond one's natural ability, one must prepare.***

PREPAREDNESS

Preparedness is primarily a responsibility of the individual.

I learned early that I had to study hard: long, focused hours of work.

- I had to know self: my strengths and weaknesses.
- I had to prepare. This meant study, education, training, getting help from those with wisdom and experience, and repeated practice to hone my skills and gain experience.

I was preparing for the opportunity when I might eventually serve and lead. It was and remains important that I ***set the example*** and that I ***be competent***. As B. C. Forbes said, "Opportunity can benefit no man who has not fitted himself to seize it and use it. Opportunity woos the worthy, shuns the unworthy. Prepare yourself to grasp opportunity, and opportunity is likely to come your way. It is not so fickle, capricious and unreasoning as some complain."[10]

OPPORTUNITY

Providing opportunity is primarily a responsibility of the leader.

It is important to prepare oneself for the prospect of opportunities that offer progress in one's journey for expanded scope of service and leadership.

I have endeavored to be competent even when assigned to a job outside my comfort zone, in which I lacked knowledge or experience. I have been blessed to have leaders who provided me opportunities to realize my full potential. This is indicative of the positive changes that have occurred in the Navy since my father entered in 1951. Among the opportunities I was afforded were those to:

- Attend and graduate from the U.S. Naval Academy Preparatory School
- Command a company of midshipmen (summer) and graduate from the U.S. Naval Academy
- Be accepted to the Navy Nuclear Propulsion Program and the U.S. Submarine Force
- Command a nuclear-powered submarine
- Command a squadron of six submarines
- Serve as second in command (chief of staff) of an aircraft carrier strike group
- Command a group of twelve submarines
- Serve as director of global operations at a joint service command responsible for several areas, including strategic deterrence, space, and cyberspace operations
- Serve as second in command of the Atlantic Fleet and fleet-wide readiness and capability needs
- Command one of the U.S. Navy's numbered fleets

While progressing in my career, I continued to seek formal education, training, and venues to practice skills that were required. When there was no dedicated time available in my career to obtain a master's degree in 1982–84, my choices of off-duty options resulted in the opportunity for me to pursue and complete that degree. This happened to be concurrent with my assignment at a joint service command. Fortuitously, later in my career a master's degree and joint service duty both became enablers for opportunity to officers who had them.

As a submarine officer, I had limited experience with aircraft carrier strike group operations. Before my assignment as chief of staff of an aircraft carrier strike group, I again had to prepare. My desire was to be competent. On my own initiative, I met with several officers who had served in that assignment. I also studied the operations and tactics and attended the carrier strike group training course in Norfolk, as well as visiting the school in San Diego.

Even during the assignment, I continually listened to experienced officers and chief petty officers. It was by chance that this job, when combined with my experience in submarines, provided a competency base for me to be considered for fleet-wide opportunities.

PERFORMANCE

> *A leader must have a vision of the future, but must also be competent and perform well to* **achieve desired effectiveness** *in realizing the vision. Day-to-day, sustained performance is the key measure of the leader's competence.*

As the years of service began to accumulate, both my required performance level and my level of competence grew in scope and breadth, but decreased in depth. I had to perform at a higher level across many subject areas, yet my technical and specific skill-set competency requirements were not as critical (that is, a mile wide and an inch deep).

Nevertheless, performance strongly influenced my future potential and the opportunities that were available. It was best for me to strive for ***excellence*** in performance during ***the job I held at the time***. I tried to ***bloom where I was planted.***

Finally, I have observed and experienced that while leaders carry out their responsibilities competently, reaffirming their vision and maintaining a strategic perspective, at the same time they must guide the urgent and important day-to-day opportunities and challenges.

When Commander Williams (right) assumed command of the *Nebraska*'s (SSBN-739) Gold crew in 1994, he became the first African American to lead a strategic ballistic-missile submarine. The ship won numerous awards for excellence and morale. (U.S. Navy)

JUDGMENT = KNOWLEDGE + EXPERIENCE

Over the years (time), I have tried to develop sound judgment by increasing my knowledge (professional reading; keeping up with current events; listening to people who have wisdom through seminars, lectures, and so on), plus increasing my experience through activities such as on-site visits to explore firsthand, practical performance of required skills and listening to chief petty officers and other experienced people.

Judgment = Knowledge + Experience, all as a function of time. The central idea is that if you work throughout the years to increase your knowledge continually, via study and remaining current in your field of endeavor, while also working to gain experience in that field, then your judgment will, accordingly, improve over time. Knowledge and experience are the drivers toward enhanced judgment, which enables a leader to better deal with uncertainty and complex situations.

- Sound judgment is essential for competent decision making.
- Decision making is a critical aspect of leadership.

Not unlike many other senior leaders, I somehow developed instincts and intuition as an extension of my judgment. These instincts and intuition are essentially feelings and a ***sense that something is right or wrong***. They have factored into my decision making.

CONTINUAL IMPROVEMENT

Early in my career, I embraced the need for continual improvement. I believed this was necessary for a leader to be competent as conditions changed, and for the organization to be effective despite changes in the local and global environment.

- *Change is a constant.* People are replaced, equipment is upgraded or degraded, technology changes, procedures are modified, the fiscal environment changes the resource situation, local and global political conditions change, and unanticipated natural and manmade events occur.
- *The status quo is a short-duration concept.* Good performance today may not be good enough in the near future as the competitive environment and conditions advance. Maintaining the status quo too long may result in regressive relative performance. Because of change, individuals and organizations are always improving or regressing over time.

  Accordingly, individuals and organizations must lead ***change toward continual improvement***, instead of slow continual regression.

continual improvement : ***Lessons from Command***

- On an individual level, personal and professional growth and continual learning are important for competence and to ***achieve desired effectiveness***.
- Experience new things.
- It is important that organizations and teams continually learn and grow together.
- Capture lessons from past and current events to help improve the future.
- Measure effectiveness (metrics) and adjust to improve.
- Analyze excellence when things go well. Determine the things that worked well and the best practices. Factor them into future events.
- Self-assessment of individual and organizational practices is a healthy evolution that should be conducted periodically. Develop a bias toward change to improve.

Father and son in the *Nebraska*'s control room, 1995. (U.S. Navy)

- Continually evaluate the local and global environments for change trends. Anticipate and adapt. Develop forward-looking plans.
- Be innovative.
- 360-degree evaluations (of self, peers, subordinates, and superiors) are helpful.
- Listen and learn from the customers (the people you serve), and those furthest from the decision-making influence base (junior people and those who are least advantaged).

Chapter Three

courage

Leadership necessitates courage in *making decisions*. Leaders should consider the facts, the opinions of a diverse group, instincts and intuition, and be decisive at the right time.

Leaders must have courage: the moral and mental strength to do what is right, even when faced with criticism or adversity. They must have the courage to make the right decisions. Courage is important.

John F. Kennedy said: "The courage of life is often a less dramatic spectacle than the courage of a final moment, but it is no less a magnificent mixture of triumph and tragedy. A man does what he must—in spite of personal consequences, in spite of obstacles and dangers and pressures—and that is the basis of all morality."[11]

Therefore, as we navigated, we found that ***courage*** was the ***third Leadership C***. Following are its key aspects:

- **accountability**
  Be responsible and accountable for your actions and conduct.

- **decisiveness**
  Have the quality of deciding; put an end to controversy. Know the facts. Do not just admire the situation. Decide to take action with a sense of urgency when needed. Know when not to make a decision.

- **initiative**
  Do what is right without orders or direction. Be innovative.

- **selflessness**
  Have, exhibit, or be motivated by little or no concern for self.

Here again we must revisit the founding principles of the Navy and Marine Corps: honor, courage, commitment, which also guide those who serve today.

COURAGE

Courage is the value that gives me the moral and mental strength to do what is right, with confidence and resolution, even in the face of temptation or adversity. This means:

- Have the courage to meet the demands of your profession.
- Make decisions and act in the best interest of the Department of the Navy and the nation, without regard to personal consequences.

- Overcome all challenges while adhering to the highest standards of personal conduct and decency.
- Be loyal to your nation by ensuring that the resources entrusted to you are used in an honest, careful, and efficient way.

[Williams SR]

ADMIRAL ELMO ZUMWALT JR.

Admiral Elmo Zumwalt Jr. was the Chief of Naval Operations from 1970 to 1974. This was a tumultuous period in our nation and in the U.S. Navy. The Vietnam War was in progress. The Cold War between the Soviet Union and United States was in full swing. Racial issues persisted in our country and the Navy. There were very few African American naval officers, and a large percentage of minority enlisted were placed in non-technical skill areas.

Admiral Zumwalt had the courage to change many things in the Navy that focused on providing equal opportunity and care for families. I had the privilege to serve as his master chief in charge of the dining facility at the Pentagon: the Secretary of the Navy and Chief of Naval Operations flag mess. I was also in the position of being one of the few African Americans assigned at the Pentagon, and close to the CNO. I took the opportunity to discuss with him my assessment of the many equal-opportunity issues that at the time persisted in the Navy.

I learned much from Admiral Zumwalt. He was a person who had courage.

COURAGE TO LEAD CHANGE: ACCOUNTABILITY, DECISIVENESS, INITIATIVE, SELFLESSNESS

During my service as a leader in the Navy, I had the privilege to contribute in a number of ways toward improving our Navy and helping others. As chief of the Pentagon dining facility for admirals and senior civilian leaders, I was one of the very few African American senior enlisted service members in proximity to senior officers. Thus I could influence change, so I stepped forward and tried to make a positive difference.

Glenn Knoblock wrote of my efforts in *Black Submariners in the United States Navy 1940-1975*: "Little did anyone know that the experiences of Melvin Williams as a young Navy steward would one day, nearly 25 years later, result in vast and important changes for the men of the steward's branch."[12]

Knoblock acknowledged the vital contribution to lasting and effective change of those who know the situation best. He wrote:

> While there can be no doubt that Admiral Zumwalt wanted to achieve racial equality in the Navy, when it came to the Steward's branch and how it should be reformed, he needed guidance and leadership from someone who was a well respected Steward, knew the ins and outs of the rate, and had a plan for implementing change in a manner that was satisfactory to all. Not surprisingly, it would take a Submarine Steward to get the job done and get it done right. While the forward-thinking actions of Admiral Elmo Zumwalt have been well documented and written about, few know that it was Master Chief Steward Melvin Williams who ended the era of the Steward in the United States Navy almost single-handedly.[13]

"Single-handedly" is of course an exaggeration, but Knoblock's thoughts do illustrate how individuals can make a difference—they just need to find in themselves the courage to step forward and do what they can.

Equal Opportunity for All Food-Service Sailors

In June 1974, as a senior chief petty officer (E-8 pay grade), I submitted my thoughts in the form of a point paper on an initiative to combine two enlisted ratings: commissary man (CS) and steward (SD). The CS rating comprised mostly Caucasian sailors who worked in a relatively respected skill area, while the SD comprised primarily minority sailors who worked in a much lesser-regarded area. The new rating would be called mess management specialist (MS). The CNO, Admiral Zumwalt, responded in a letter dated 14 June 1974:

> Dear Senior Chief Williams,
>
> I would like to take this opportunity to commend you for the proposals you recently submitted concerning the merger of the CS/SD ratings. Although the merger is designed to provide a broader career field for personnel serving in the food management areas, I am in complete agreement with you that implementation should not adversely affect career personnel currently in the SD rating.
>
> In view of the potential problems which you have identified, I have forwarded your recommendations to the Chief of Naval Personnel for review and further study. . . . I appreciate your concern on this issue and thank you, once again, for your comments and recommendations.[14]

That December, the CNO made the decision to merge the CS and SD ratings. The net effect was to end discrimination that had been occurring in the primarily minority steward rating and, eventually, to create equal opportunity for all sailors who served in the new mess management specialist rating.

Better Conditions for Naval Academy Stewards

In November 1974, I and two others forwarded to Navy leadership an extensive memorandum. We proposed significant changes to the working and living conditions of the enlisted stewards, primarily African American and Filipino, who served at the premiere institution for development of future U.S. naval officers, the Naval Academy. The action led to several positive changes, which Mel Jr., who entered as a midshipman in July 1974, was able to witness.

Vice Admiral David H. Bagley, Deputy Chief of Naval Operations, explained the need for these changes in a 4 January 1975 memo to the Academy's superintendent: "During the early August 1974 briefings presented within the Bureau of Naval Personnel regarding the merger of the Steward (SD) and Commissary-man (CS) ratings, comment was made concerning the overall situation of SD personnel at the U.S. Naval Academy, and in particular, alluded to unresponsiveness toward their well-being and upward mobility."

Such wording would be far more unusual today, when equal opportunity for all has been established officially as a given. But from the 1950s through the 1970s, major societal shifts were in full swing.

Combined with "much congressional pressure and high level interest," as Bagley described the political atmosphere, our memo offered firsthand evidence from our personal review of the situation. Collectively, this proof and willingness helped to produce the outcome: "In support of our human goals program," wrote Bagley, "positive action must be taken by each command to prevent/alleviate practices, however covert, detrimental to minority personnel and to reemphasize that each individual has infinite dignity and worth."[15]

Equal Opportunity in the Senior Enlisted Ranks

In August 1976, I forwarded another extensive memorandum to Navy leaders. This proposed initiatives to provide equal opportunity for all people, including minorities and women (of whom there were few at the top) to be eligible for serving as master chief of the force. The idea was to demonstrate that a minority and/or woman could and should have the opportunity to be selected as the top enlisted leader of the surface community, the aviation community, the submarine community, and so on.

"The lack of serious minority consideration in the recent Supply System Command MCPOF selection process," I wrote, "not only raises doubt as to its credibility, but also intensifies the perception that qualified minority members are not afforded an equal opportunity to compete for this senior enlisted position."

Written at a time when the Navy's nineteenth-century attitudes toward enlisted personnel—especially minority enlisted personnel—were slowly being updated, memos such as these "worked from the inside" to help maintain the impetus.

"To what extent is the Supply Systems Command committed to equal opportunity?" I asked. "This issue is important to me as an individual and as a Navy person. I raise the question both in support of the Navy's Equal Opportunity programs and to reinforce my waning troth."[16]

The Chief of Naval Operations, then Admiral James L. Holloway III, accepted the recommendations for action, and positive changes were eventually realized in the Navy. In 1976, the equivalent of today's Director of the Navy Staff noted in an endorsement of the recommendations: "I have worked closely with Master Chief

Williams for the year I have served in my present assignment. My evaluation of this man is he is one of the finest, most dedicated, conscientious petty officers I have ever known. His quiet, unassuming nature only lends credence to the sincerity of his comments in this letter. This is a sincere man asking us some good questions."[17]

I had laid the groundwork for such positive feedback to my suggestions over many years, as part of an ongoing effort to help improve not only my own situation, but that of everyone under my charge. This is a critical aspect of leadership, one that needs to be cultivated with purpose and focus. Lieutenant (jg) S. F. St. Thomas had noted and commended this attitude the previous March: "He has directed the operations of the Secretary of the Navy–Chief of Naval Operations Flag Mess conscientiously, skillfully utilizing the limited number of personnel to take full advantage of the special skills that each subordinate brings to his work. He ensures excellent results by nurturing a sense of pride and confidence in his subordinates, who respond enthusiastically to his leadership."[18]

Lieutenant (jg) St. Thomas's letter could serve as a list of characteristics to develop for anyone who is studying the art of leading others. He went on: "Constantly working in close proximity to the most senior military and civilian members of the Navy, Master Chief Williams has consistently demonstrated courtesy and thoughtfulness of speech, and serenity under pressure. He thinks and acts deliberately and precisely. His uniforms are maintained in a meticulous manner."

Carefully considered delegation of tasks to subordinates, maximizing each one's strong points while encouraging through a positive attitude and confidence, expecting the best of everyone and demonstrating it yourself, including in your dress and speech—all of these are central to effective leadership.

Command Master Chief at Sea: Serving and Leading Sailors

After serving on the presidential yacht for one year and with the Secretary of the Navy and Chief of Naval Operations in the Pentagon for seven years, I requested to go back to sea for my final assignment. So in 1977, as command master chief of a large surface ship, the destroyer tender *Piedmont*, I could see for myself whether the equal-opportunity changes were taking place. (This is an example of accountability.)

I observed that the cultural change associated with the rating merger was slow. As the *Piedmont*'s command master chief, I was invited to attend a seminar to review the status of the newly created MS rating. We assessed that it was having problems due to the high dropout rate of former commissary men who indicated they wanted no part of former stewards' duties.

So I submitted to the Navy Food Service Office a "Communications and Training Plan" (a point paper) regarding the rating merger, to help institute cultural change. I included analysis and recommendations for improving recruiting, incentives, training, enforcement of guidelines, and methods to enhance the real and perceived image of those who served in the new MS rating.

The plan was accepted. Over the course of many months, most of the recommendations were implemented, and the MS rating eventually evolved into one that was respected. A person of any background who desired to gain expertise in food service and hotel management (through experience in managing barracks and military living quarters) could excel through the MS rating.

I had many opportunities, as command master chief, to help develop and encourage junior sailors. I also had many occasions to shape officers' thinking. It was a challenging, yet gratifying, final tour of duty.

Naming a Destroyer for a Navy Steward

In March 1999, on behalf of our former Navy stewards' group, Units K-West and B-East U.S. Navy Mess Attendants Association (named for the Norfolk, Virginia, school barracks assigned to stewards in 1932), I wrote a letter to Secretary of the Navy Richard Danzig. I requested that he consider naming a U.S. Navy destroyer to honor former Navy steward William Pinckney, one of the few African American sailors to earn the Navy Cross during World War II.

In October 1942, the carrier *Enterprise* (CV-6), the Big E, was bombed during the Battle of Santa Cruz (but survived and went on to inflict yet more damage on a weakening enemy). Ship's Cook Third Class Pinckney pulled another survivor to safety before making his own way through the burning wreckage. He lived until 1976.

My letter read as follows.

March 2, 1999
The Honorable Richard Danzig
Secretary of the Navy
Room 4-E-686
Pentagon
Arlington, VA 20350-1000

Dear Mr. Secretary:

Attached to this letter is a copy of a request to Senator Strom Thurmond of South Carolina, urging his support for the naming of a United States Navy destroyer or frigate in honor of Ex-Officer's Steward William Pinckney, USN, Navy Cross recipient during World War II.

As a member of the units K-West and B-East Mess Attendants Association, a master chief petty officer retiree (Leading Chief, SEC-NAV/CNO Flag Mess 1968–76), father to an active duty Navy captain and grandfather to an active duty Marine Corps captain, I am requesting that you make the nomination to name a vessel in memory of our departed shipmate and naval hero William Pinckney.

The attachments to this letter support the legitimacy of Pinckney's actions, however some members of our organization who actually knew him, and all of us who know about him, would be thrilled and honored to attend a christening of his namesake before we pass on through this life.

For your information, our organization was recently recognized during a dedication ceremony at Arlington Cemetery on September 18, 1998. In attendance were Admirals Paul Reason, Commander U.S. Atlantic Fleet; Rear Admiral Christopher Weaver, Commandant, U.S. Naval District, Washington, D.C.; and, both Retired, Vice Admiral Samuel Gravely and Rear Admiral Benjamin Hacker. We were also in receipt of greetings from your predecessor, John H. Dalton.

As I have now played all of my cards in this respect, I and my organization Shipmates will continue to offer prayers in the memory of William Pinckney, with the hope that you will have the opportunity to give his name a lasting naval honor.

Very respectfully yours,
Melvin G. Williams, Sr., MSCM (SS)
USN, Retired

Our initiative was accepted. The construction keel of the guided-missile destroyer USS *William Pinckney* (DDG-91) was laid

Master Chief Williams is a member of the Units K-West and B-East U.S. Navy Mess Attendants Association. The group's name refers to the barracks locations assigned to stewards at school in Norfolk, Virginia, starting in 1932. Historical markers have been placed in significant locations such as this one in Norfolk—across the street from the headquarters of Commander, U.S. Second Fleet, where Vice Admiral Williams served. (Courtesy of the authors)

in July 2001. The ship was commissioned in May 2004; she and her crew serve our nation and Navy today.

Historical Markers Recognizing Sailor Contributions

Along with other members of our former stewards' group, I was able to work within government to establish historical markers recognizing and honoring sailors who served before us. We placed markers at the following locations:

- USS *North Carolina* Battleship Museum, noting contributions of former stewards
- Dining facility of the U.S. Naval Academy, honoring thousands of stewards who served our future naval leaders
- Site of the former stewards' school in Norfolk, Virginia
- Arlington Cemetery

> A leader must have courage: the moral and mental strength to do what is right, even when faced with criticism or adversity.

Throughout history, the men and women who serve in the armed forces in defense of freedom, human rights, and the rule of law have been leaders who routinely demonstrate courage. We, the beneficiaries of freedom, should be grateful to these courageous leaders. I am.

EARLY YEARS: DEFEND YOURSELF!

A lesson regarding courage occurred for me when I was nine years old. We had recently moved to a new neighborhood. A young boy about my age, but much larger, called me a name I did not appreciate. I scurried into our home and explained the situation to my mother. Dad was at sea.

In a nice but deliberate way, Mom directed me to go back outside and defend myself. I do not, in retrospect, believe she wanted me to fight. I do believe she wanted me to have the courage to stand up for my honor—after all, my name is Melvin and not the name the boy called me.

A fight ensued. Visualize a cartoon fight with two characters swirling in a tornado cloud of arms and legs. That was us. After what seemed an eternity—really it was about thirty seconds—we agreed to stop fighting. I do not recall any actual blows landing on either of us. Nevertheless, we were both exhausted. He agreed to call me Melvin, and I agreed to call him by his name. We became best friends. Mom was not pleased by the fighting, but she was satisfied that I had demonstrated courage.

ACCOUNTABILITY

"Stuff happens." But in my view, leaders should be accountable for the organization's effectiveness and the decisions made toward this end. ***Making the right decisions requires courage.***

As Dr. Martin Luther King Jr. said, "The ultimate measure of a man is not where he stands in moments of comfort and convenience, but where he stands at times of challenge and controversy."[19]

Humans are fallible. When I have fallen short in my conduct, I have endeavored to correct the situation and admit mistakes. This can be humbling. But it is the right thing to do.

Many times during my career, I found myself standing alone explaining to superiors why and how mistakes were made, and what I would do to prevent recurrence in the future. I had to explain my decisions.

Also, many times I found myself standing alone explaining to the team why and how I had fallen short in leading the team's efforts—but also how we would improve going forward.

In the armed forces, leaders must often stand alone before the families of service members who have paid the ultimate sacrifice, or suffered the wounds of war and service.

Again, these are humbling experiences that require courage. In the world today, I believe it will benefit people—as well as leaders' credibility and the tradition of leadership itself—if we all consistently demonstrate the courage to be personally accountable when "stuff happens."

Leaders should ***set the example*** of personal and professional conduct. This takes effort. We are watched and scrutinized. In my opinion, this is appropriate because of the privileges that are sometimes granted to leaders, and because of the significant scope of leaders' responsibilities. We should be accountable.

When desired organizational effectiveness is achieved and things go well, it is best to attribute the success to the individuals who most contributed, and to the collective team. This is not a new concept.

A COMMAND EXPERIENCE

The command was performing well, generally slightly above the average performance of comparable commands. Then one evening while at sea and submerged in our submarine, an unexpected, untoward event occurred. Although no one was hurt and there was no damage, this was a performance concern for which I felt personally accountable.

At sea and submerged is the natural condition for a submarine while performing its military mission. Ever since the beginning of the U.S. Submarine Force in 1900 with the purchase of the USS *Hol-*

land (SS-1), submarines and their crews, submariners, have served courageously in this potentially hostile submerged environment.

If a human error is made, if an equipment malfunction occurs, or if an adversary initiates hostile action, the lives of the entire crew may be in jeopardy. Accordingly, the level of training, education, and professionalism required of volunteers serving in the U.S. Submarine Force is among the highest in our armed forces.

In our crew that evening, a mistake was made. We took appropriate actions and later returned safely to home port on completion of the mission. I accepted responsibility for the event and was accountable to my superiors and the crew. Joseph Conrad is widely believed to have said: "In each ship there is one man who, in the hour of emergency or peril at sea, can turn to no other man. There is one who alone is ultimately responsible for the safe navigation, engineering performance, accurate gunfire and morale of his ship. He is the Commanding Officer."

Once in home port, I saw this event as an opportunity to improve our overall effectiveness and performance. It was a defining moment for me in the command assignment.

With the commitment of the officers, chief petty officers, and crew, we resolved to do better. Over the next year the command achieved many accolades, including top-performing strategic ballistic-missile submarine in the squadron, fleet, and nation.

I had held myself accountable for the mistake—and the crew went on to achieve higher effectiveness and performance. It was a privilege to serve with them.

DECISIVENESS

As noted earlier, decision making is an essential element of leadership. It takes courage to make the right decisions. Much has been written about the factors to be considered in this process. In my experience, the following considerations have been particularly useful.

decision making

- Consider fundamental principles.
- Know the facts, but do not wait for perfect clarity.
- Obtain thoughts, recommendations, and opinions from a diverse group of advisers. Ask for and encourage dissenting views.
- Consider the decision's effect on the wider, more complex system. This includes consequences for people and for overall effectiveness.
- Consider precedents and the associated effectiveness of similar decisions.
- Understand reality. Understand perception.
- Take into consideration your instinct and intuition, as appropriate.
- Consider that as leader, you are accountable.
- Decide, communicate, and act with a sense of urgency. Assess. Adapt as appropriate.
- Know when *not* to make a decision—which is, in fact, a decision.

KNOWING WHEN NOT TO MAKE A DECISION

Being decisive takes courage. That said, I join other leaders who believe there are times when *not* making a decision is a deliberate option that may be the right thing to do at the moment.

Early during my career, I began chewing on an unlighted pipe, a habit picked up by observing my father and his friends back in the late 1960s. The pipe is essentially a pacifier. Eventually it became a leadership tool for me, helping me to refrain from making decisions that my lesser experienced people would eventually be able to make. It facilitated professional development and growth for my people.

As a more experienced officer, I could reach conclusions and make decisions much faster than many of my officers and staff. Chewing on the pipe kept my mouth shut, permitted assessments and deliberation, and sometimes allowed small mistakes. Although I was accountable for the time delays and occasional minor errors, I found that my officers and staff were better able to grow, learn, and gain experience in decision making and leadership. I did, of course, intervene or decide if safety or the mission effectiveness were in jeopardy.

I recall one day at sea, submerged on our submarine, we were conducting high-speed maneuvers. As commanding officer, I observed one of my junior officers as he drove the submarine by giving the crew the necessary orders. The officer of the deck ordered, "Right full rudder," to steer the ship to the right, just as in a scene from *The Hunt for Red October*.

As I listened to my junior officer give this order, I quietly maintained a vise-grip clamp on my pipe. The problem was, he should have ordered "Left full rudder"!

I waited "patiently" for him to correct himself—to no avail. Finally I intervened by suggesting that he shift the direction of the rudder to the left.

His response was, in an excited voice, "My bad! Left full rudder!"

I thought, This is not an expression that we in the older generation would use in a tense military situation. Nevertheless, he learned from his mistake.

I retain the unlighted pipe today. It has many deep teeth marks!

INITIATIVE

Formulating and instituting new approaches takes courage. It requires challenging assumptions. It is necessary to influence people who may be comfortable with the status quo and conventional wisdom.

History is populated with courageous people who have taken an innovative approach—and, without guidance, direction, or orders from above, changed the way in which we live, for the better.

A common trait that my father and I share is the modicum of courage needed to seize the initiative. We can both offer numerous examples of ways in which we were able to work with others to try new approaches—toward improvement.

It raises our ***competitive spirit*** when someone proclaims, "It has always been that way." As Ralph Waldo Emerson stated: "Whatever course you decide upon, there is always someone to tell you that you are wrong. There are always difficulties arising which tempt you to believe that your critics are right. To map out a course of action and follow it to an end requires . . . courage."[20]

As I think about the positive changes my father initiated for stewards at the U.S. Naval Academy while I was a midshipman, I recall the spirits of black and Filipino stewards being uplifted. During my four years there, I observed stewards being better treated while midshipmen's attitudes toward them improved.

This is an important leadership point: As midshipmen graduate and enter the fleet as young officers, they must treat all people with dignity and respect, regardless of background, culture, gender, or race.

SELFLESSNESS

Selflessness is a leadership trait that requires courage and a genuine commitment to the well-being of others. This is an implied trait of Robert Greenleaf's servant leader.

Not unlike many other leaders, I have had many opportunities to serve, support, defend, and protect others despite the consequences to self. Selflessness, when inculcated within each person in the organization, helps the leader to create an atmosphere of teamwork and the cohesion necessary to achieve desired effectiveness.

Chapter Four

commitment

A commitment to *developing people* is essential. The better prepared a team's individuals are for achieving the desired effectiveness, the higher the chances of success. This means providing opportunity for them to realize their full potential. The leader must be capable of trusting others, which necessitates accepting risks associated with delegating authority, and permitting some mistakes by those gaining experience. Developing people means providing for education, training, and mentoring. Developing current and future leaders is a leader's responsibility.

We believe that each individual and leader must make a commitment to something greater than self. This is not a revelation, but simply our affirmation based on our experiences. Commitment is important. One of our nation's forefathers, Thomas Paine, said:

"Those who expect to reap the blessings of freedom, must, like men, undergo the fatigue of supporting it."[21]

We were and are committed to service to nation through leadership in the U.S. Navy. The philosopher Aristotle noted: "Excellence is an art won by training and habituation. We do not act rightly because we have written virtue or excellence, but we rather have those because we have acted rightly. We are what we repeatedly do. Excellence, then, is not an act but a habit."[22]

We have a commitment to excellence. We have endeavored to make it a habit. Leaders must have a commitment to developing people. The ***fourth Leadership C*** that we identified as we navigated was ***commitment***. Its key aspects are:

- **service**

  A commitment to serving and supporting something greater than self; in our case, defending freedom through service in the Navy. Commitment involves the leadership responsibility of ***developing people*** and serving their needs in terms of resources (people, money, time). Apportion time to serve and support others.

- **excellence**

  A commitment to excellence is a must. We believe that "excellence is continually doing the right things right."[23] Have high standards. There is no room for mediocrity. Set the example. A commitment to excellence requires hard work.

- **goals**

  Develop and commit to achieving goals. This requires

focus. Do not fear failure when developing or pursuing goals.

- **teamwork**
  Have a commitment to the team. Develop loyalty.

Here again, the core values are at the heart of the discussion: honor, courage, commitment. Again they are relevant regardless of one's occupation, leadership situation, culture, and gender.

COMMITMENT

The day-to-day duty of every man and woman in the Department of the Navy is to join together as a team to improve the quality of our work, our people, and ourselves. Resolve to:

- Foster respect up and down the chain of command.
- Care for the personal and spiritual well-being of your people.
- Show respect toward all people without regard to race, religion, or gender.
- Strive always for positive change and personal improvement.
- Exhibit the highest degree of moral character, professional excellence, quality, and competence in all that you do.

[Williams SR]

SERVICE

Military life was difficult, but I believed I would be okay as long as my family was taken care of. Back in the 1950s, as an African American sailor, I was lucky to initially serve in the Navy on the more socially liberal West Coast of the United States, in California. Ruth and I both knew that our Navy life was a choice—including the good, the bad, and the ugly.

The good was having a sense of security and service because we were a part of something bigger than ourselves, which brought with it a sense of dignity and respect. We made the commitment to service.

The bad was trying to support a wife and four children on the pay of a third-class petty officer, at the time earning about $160 per month. Accordingly, I had to work many part-time jobs on the side. This included serving as a caterer, bartender, waiter, and cook. We made it through.

The ugly was being transferred to the deep South during the heat of the Civil Rights movement. Our children left good schools in San Diego to attend poor, segregated schools in New Orleans. Ruth and I found ourselves attempting to explain to our young kids about segregation and discrimination.

Our youngest son, Kenneth, was born late in the day on 12 November 1960 at the U.S. Public Service Hospital in New Orleans. Two days later, with Ruth and the baby still in the hospital, I donned my Navy uniform and headed there to visit them—only to be delayed by an angry crowd yelling, "Two, four, six, eight, we don't want to integrate!" Six-year-old Ruby Bridges entered school accompanied by U.S. marshals who later noted how brave she was, never even whimpering. Ruby became an example for the Civil Rights movement. Her image was captured by Norman Rockwell, my favorite illustrator. I have a copy of it—*The Problem We All Live With*—in our home.

I started my Navy career in 1951. Fourteen of my first seventeen years were on sea duty, starting with the aircraft carrier USS *Hancock* (CVA-19). I transitioned to the surface fleet on board USS *Dixie* (AD-14), USS *Prairie* (AD-15), and the destroyer USS *Hollister* (DD-788).

After ten years of aircraft carrier and surface service, I volunteered to serve in submarines. I wanted to try something new—a new challenge. I earned my Silver Dolphins as a qualified submariner in early 1962, on board the USS *Carp* (SS-338). My other assignments included the *Thomas Jefferson*, *Entemedor* (SS-340), *James K. Polk* (Blue crew), and Submarine Squadron Ten on board the USS *Fulton* (AS-11). It felt good to be an intimate part of a submarine crew. These crews were tops in esprit de corps and camaraderie.

EXCELLENCE

Excellence has always been my standard for performance. It started with self. I wanted to set the example through my own performance. One of the visible performance factors during my time in the Navy was how my uniform looked. I worked to keep my uniform "squared away," including a fresh shine on my black leather shoes. This was a visible demonstration of my commitment to excellence as the standard.

I worked hard to ensure that my day-to-day performance reflected the highest standard. This commitment was eventually documented in my performance evaluations, and it contributed to my advancement opportunity.

It was a point of honor to be awarded the Navy's Good Conduct Medal repeatedly throughout my career. The many Good Conduct Medals on my uniform served to communicate to my junior sailors where the bar was set with respect to conduct and performance.

After eleven years of service on aircraft carriers and surface ships, Steward Second Class Williams earned his Silver Dolphins as a qualified submariner in 1962, on board the USS *Carp* (SS-338). (U.S. Navy)

GOALS

My goals were:

- As a single man, join the U.S. Navy to serve our country, while at the same time earning an income, learning, and traveling
- As a married man, take care of my family
- Determine what I could do to make the Navy better

Like many young people, I wanted to get out of the home environment and learn new things. The Navy provided an opportunity to serve and develop. After marrying in 1953, I worked to ensure that I provided for my family. I felt that as long as they were secure during my Navy travels and deployments, I could focus on thoughts aligned with General George Patton's when he stated, "I am a soldier, I fight where I am told, and I win where I fight."

I believed in taking pride in my work. And as I served on aircraft carriers, surface ships, and submarines, I looked for ways to improve things. I truly was trying to help make the Navy better. As my service time accumulated, I developed as a leader and was better able to have influence on some conditions in the command in which I served, as well as in the Navy overall.

TEAMWORK

I could share countless sea stories that describe the value and importance of teamwork. In the business of food service, hundreds of hard-working and hungry sailors look to you and your team to serve a high-quality meal that can be consumed in a relatively short period, due to the nature of operations at sea.

Our food-service team continually had to factor in customer desires and synchronize actions in preparation of each of the many meals served throughout every day. Our output had a significant

In the mid-1950s during the Cold War, the *Hancock* (CVA-19), Steward Seaman Williams's first ship, became the first aircraft carrier to be successfully configured for aircraft launches using steam catapults. (U.S. Navy)

effect on the crew's morale. We worked together to ensure only the best for our crew.

I have been privileged to serve on several high-performing teams where there was true commitment. I continue to learn from these experiences. Following are some examples of this teamwork.

Korean War: During this period I served ashore at Naval Air Station El Centro, California. We demonstrated good teamwork and commitment supporting naval aviators who eventually operated overseas in the war. In food service we took our jobs seriously, knowing that quality meals served with a smile was our way of supporting these warriors headed for the front lines. Although I was relatively junior at the time, I felt a sense of purpose and commitment to the Navy and the nation. All of us who served during that time earned the Korean Service Ribbon.

Vietnam War: My service on board the *Hollister* included good teamwork during missions off Korea and Formosa (Taiwan) that preceded the Vietnam War. I enjoyed my time on a Navy destroyer. The ship was small in the large oceans and seas, and the at-sea deployment periods long. Our crew worked together to ensure that we were ready for any assigned mission. Our food-service team kept everyone fed with the best quality chow available at the time. Accordingly, the crew was happy and performed well.

Cold War: During my time on board the *Hancock*, we became the first aircraft carrier to be configured successfully to launch aircraft using steam catapults. We also supported testing of the Regulus missile, an early predecessor of the Tomahawk cruise missile that Mel Jr.'s submarine later launched.

Chief of Naval Operations Admiral Elmo Zumwalt (left) was the first senior Navy leader to drive equal opportunity for all who served. Key changes under his leadership increased possibilities for minorities and women. Senior Chief Williams stands in the second row facing Zumwalt, ca. 1973. (U.S. Navy)

On board the *Carp*, we were ordered to support potential hostilities against the Soviet Union during the Cuban Missile Crisis in October 1962. This was a tense period for the nation and the Navy. History identifies this crisis as being the closest mankind has come to executing nuclear warfare on a large scale. Our small diesel-powered, fast-attack submarine did its part to support a positive outcome.

Also, in the 1960s, I thoroughly enjoyed the work and the camaraderie on board the strategic ballistic missile submarines *Thomas Jefferson* and *James K. Polk*. Teamwork was strong, with the crews close and professional, as we made successful strategic deterrence patrols. These were key turning points in my career.

We had high priority for Navy resources, due to the importance of our mission. Our food-service quality was renowned as among the best in the Navy. On one patrol, I arranged to have a special dinner for which all crew members had to dress in costume, including funny hats. During dinner, a higher authority called for an unexpected readiness exercise—which required the crew to quickly assume battle-station positions in the submarine for a simulated missile launch. It was quite amusing to see the captain, chief of the boat, and crew at their stations wearing those hats and costumes!

In 1973, Senior Chief Williams served as leading chief for the Secretary of the Navy and Chief of Naval Operations flag mess at the Pentagon. He shakes hands here with Secretary of the Navy John Warner. (U.S. Navy)

[Williams JR]

Commitment is an intangible thing that enables individuals and organizations to achieve high performance and desired effectiveness despite the challenges and obstacles that inevitably occur.

Each individual and each leader should make a commitment to something greater than self.

Having a purpose, and a commitment to that purpose, has been important to me. My purpose and passion are to serve others through leadership. The notion of commitment to something greater than self has the deliberate effect of benefiting society in an overall sense, one's nation, or a cause that ideally supports a universal truth or principle.

SERVICE

My father and I have a commitment to the defense of freedom through service in the Navy. This has been the case for nearly sixty consecutive years of active-duty service. It has been by choice.

As our nation's leaders and military leaders of an all-volunteer armed force endeavor to create a ***sense of service*** among our younger generations, the notion of commitment to something greater than self is particularly germane. The leader Dr. Albert Schweitzer said to his followers: "I don't know what your destiny will be, but one thing I know: the only ones among you who will be really happy are those who will have sought and found how to serve."[24]

In the Williams definition of leadership, we include serving needs. Leaders must be committed to providing the day-to-day resources—people, money, time—that their people need to be successful in achieving desired effectiveness. I have observed that some leaders and organizations have a mismatch between commitment in words and commitment in required resources. Eliminating this is essential to a leader's responsibility to serve needs. It also better enables followers to be committed to effectiveness and the leader's vision.

During my military career, I too occasionally fell short in this area, but I continued to align commitment in words to resource allocation for my people. In today's fiscally challenged environment, I committed to filling resource needs. Then, if I was unable to do so, I stopped the commitment in words, thereby eliminating the mismatch. I preferred to inform our people that we just could not get the resources, and we had to move on.

After my military career, I will doubtless continue to serve others in a leadership capacity. Serving and helping others is important.

Leaders must make a commitment and take action toward developing people. This provides a wonderful return on investment—you watch others develop, learn, and progress toward the realization of their full potential. As Booker T. Washington noted: "Few things help an individual more than to place responsibility upon him, and to let him know that you trust him."[25]

EXCELLENCE

A commitment to excellence is a must.

Leaders should establish excellence as the standard for performance. It requires hard work. This has been the case for me during leadership assignments. During command, on any particular day some mistakes were made. Nevertheless, our team knew that excellence was the overall standard. They knew there was no room for mediocrity. We assessed and learned from the mistakes. We continually improved, with the day-to-day performance bar set high.

Over time it became a habit. This was not forced or dictated. The chief petty officers, officers, and crew were committed to excellence and continual improvement. It was a joy to watch.

We believe that excellence is ***continually doing the right things right***. For me and my commands, this has been applied as follows:

Continually: A consistent level of effort was involved, which created habits. The effort was not for just one at-sea period, one deployment, or one annual performance-evaluation period by individuals. Continual implied sustained and for the long haul. And implied in the level of effort was commitment.

Doing: This meant taking action—not just sending emails or attending meetings, but delivering product and measurable results toward the desired effectiveness.

Will Rogers said: "Even though you are on the right track, you'll get run over if you just sit there."[26] Doing involved communicating to achieve understanding and commitment at all levels. It required accountability. It necessitated self-assessment and feedback, with metrics and measurements. Otherwise the doing was labor lost and we fell short.

The right things: Leaders should determine the right things for the organization to accomplish, because they must have a vision for the organization. Individuals must determine the right things for personal excellence.

We identified our priorities, goals, and objectives, and modified them over time as required by internal and external change. The right things were inextricably linked to the commander's desired effectiveness and vision.

Right: This referred to doing the right things in a principled way, correctly and consistently with our values, ethics, and the high standards of excellence.

During my command assignments, our people continually did the right things right. I was blessed.

GOALS

With a commitment to service and to excellence as the standard, a commitment to goals is essential. These are linked to the larger mission accomplishment, desired effectiveness, and realization of the leader's vision. As an individual, goals are linked to realizing your full potential.

My personal goals during the early years were to:

- Defend freedom by serving in the U.S. Navy. This was based on observing my father.
- Become a naval officer by attending the U.S. Naval Academy. I wanted to be a leader and have the responsibility to serve and help other people develop. I believed that as an officer, I would have the opportunity to serve a larger group of people. I pursued acceptance to the U.S. Naval Academy because I believed this was the most challenging and best path to becoming a naval officer.
- Become a nuclear-engineer-trained submarine officer. I was exposed to the exciting world of submarines by observing my father and his friends. I also believed that to become a "nuke" and a submariner were among the most demanding and challenging options for a naval officer. The challenge appealed to me.
- As a married man, take care of my family.

Do not fear failure when determining goals. They should be measurable and achievable, but not self-limiting due to fear of failure.

During career assignments, we identified specific and measurable goals and focus areas for the organization that linked to where we wanted to be (vision), who we were (purpose), and how we wanted to perform in achieving positive results and output (desired effectiveness). We experienced that it was a true win-win situation to ***align individuals' personal goals with the organization's goals.***

TEAMWORK

In the Williams definition of leadership, we include creating teamwork. This means that leaders must be committed to building the relationships based on caring and trust that are necessary for organizational cohesion.

When there is trust, teamwork is possible. When individuals are committed and loyal to the team, the potential for success is high.

Like my father, I have had the privilege of serving on several high-performing teams whose members were truly committed. I am still learning from these experiences. Following are examples of effective teamwork.

Cold War: During the Cold War between the United States and former Soviet Union, the 1980s submarine crews of the USS *Jack* (SSN-605) and USS *Woodrow Wilson* (SSBN-624, Gold crew) exhibited teamwork.

My first operational assignment in the Navy was as a division officer on board the fast-attack submarine *Jack*, in 1980. As an ensign who had recently completed Navy nuclear propulsion and submarine officer training, I traveled to a port near the Mediterranean Sea (one of the Seven Seas) and reported to the *Jack*, which was already there on deployment. Its mission was aligned with the standard nature of Cold War operations.

I soon realized that I happened to be the only African American officer on board. Additionally, there were very few African American enlisted crew members. Nevertheless, I made it a point to focus on people, developing personal but professional relationships with my divisional sailors, the chief petty officers on the submarine, and my fellow officers. It was through establishment of these relationships, combined with hard work and study, that I was able to complete initial submarine qualifications faster than my contemporaries. The crew helped me quite a bit.

I learned about the art and science of submarining from my first commanding officer, Commander Dick Hartman. He was a good leader. As a result of teamwork, the ship went on to earn the Navy Unit Commendation for extraordinary performance. "The superb crew morale maintained during an extended period at sea in the stressful Mediterranean environment reflected outstanding leadership at all levels," wrote Secretary of the Navy John Lehman of our service in the *Jack*.[27]

In 1984, I reported to the strategic ballistic-missile submarine *Woodrow Wilson* as the chief engineer officer. This was a pivotal assignment in my leadership development; my position on this submarine was responsible to the commanding officer for not only the safe and proper operation of the propulsion plant and auxiliary systems, but also for leading and developing about 60 percent of the crew.

As I reported on board, I again noted that I happened to be the only African American officer, once again with few African American enlisted crew members. My commanding officer was Captain K. T. Hoephner, a superb submarine officer and leader of people.

Because he allowed me to run the engineering department, I was able to grow and learn as a leader.

Our teamwork on the *Woodrow Wilson* earned the ship the top engineering award, the top battle-efficiency award, the top award for retaining and taking care of people, and the Navy's Meritorious Unit Commendation for outstanding performance. The citation, addressed to officers and enlisted personnel, commended our service "in connection with Fleet Ballistic Missile deterrent patrols 63 through 70 conducted from 1 January 1985 to 28 January 1987," for excelling "in every aspect of submarining from near perfect strategies and tactical readiness to Engineering excellence. In addition to her operational expertise, USS *Woodrow Wilson* distinguished itself in retention, earning the Golden Anchor Award for 1986."[28]

Operation Desert Storm: The teamwork demonstrated by the submarine crew of the USS *Louisville* (SSN-724) resulted in the first combat strikes that a U.S. nuclear submarine had ever made, during the initial attacks of Operation Desert Storm, 19 January 1991.

I reported on board this fast-attack submarine in 1989, as the executive officer (second in command). I served with three different commanding officers and all were good, albeit different in their leadership styles. This assignment was the key opportunity through which I was able to learn three distinct approaches to leadership.

Commander Frank Stewart was my second commanding officer. He ably led the crew into combat at the onset of the coalition war against Saddam Hussein during Desert Storm. The *Louisville* had been scheduled to go on a deployment consistent with previous Cold War missions, and had received a short-notice assignment in December 1990 to travel from San Diego, the submarine's homeport, to the Red Sea (one of the Seven Seas) at best speed.

Because he had innovative ideas, Commander Stewart worked with the submarine-force leadership to have a temporary, yet more effective navigation support device installed on the *Louisville*. As it turned out, this relatively new (back in late 1990) Global Positioning System device enabled the submarine to travel the 14,000-plus nautical miles at record speed, while also maintaining navigation accuracy. Thus I learned about innovation.

Because the executive officer is also the ship's training officer, we had to work as a team to be fully ready for the first-ever submarine Tomahawk strike mission. This would also be the first time a U.S. nuclear-powered submarine would conduct combat firings. World War II was the last time U.S. diesel-powered submarines had been engaged in battle.

During the *Louisville*'s high-speed transit to the Red Sea, many episodes of teamwork and individual accomplishment occurred, classified stories that ultimately led to successful combat strikes on 19 January 1991 in support of the coalition efforts. Our team went on to earn the top battle-efficiency award and the Navy Unit Commendation.

The *Louisville* was commended on a "job well done" for our "highly successful support of Operation Desert Storm."[29]

Strategic Deterrence: The crews of the USS *Nebraska* showed extraordinary teamwork from 1994 to 1997. In 1996 they were the top-performing strategic-missile unit in the nation. Strategic ballistic-missile submarines play a critical role in our ability to deter potential adversaries from employing weapons of mass destruction. This is strategic deterrence.

These submarines are silently at sea every day. To keep each sub platform at sea for a higher percentage of time, two separate crews are needed (designated Blue crew and Gold crew). One is

As executive officer on board the USS *Louisville* (SSN-724), Commander Williams helped lead the teamwork that resulted in the ship's being the first U.S. nuclear submarine to strike in combat. (U.S. Navy)

actually at sea (on patrol), and the other crew is on rest, then training for the next at-sea period.

In 1994, my counterpart, Commander Bill Hendrickson, and I had the privilege of becoming two of the first officers of commander rank (O-5) to be assigned to command an *Ohio*-class (Trident) strategic ballistic-missile submarine. Since their introduction in the early 1980s, these commands had been designated major command and been assigned to second-tour officers of captain rank (O-6).

So as junior commanders on the waterfront in Kings Bay, Georgia, with the more senior captains in charge of the other submarines, Bill Hendrickson assumed command of the *Nebraska*'s Blue crew and I of the Gold (whereby I also happened to become the first African American to command a strategic ballistic-missile submarine).

During our three years leading our respective crews, there was significant teamwork and effectiveness. On short notice during my first patrol, our Gold crew was tasked to shoot two Trident D5 missiles (reconfigured with test systems). This was successful. During the five patrols with the *Nebraska*'s Gold crew (and while teaming with the Blue crew), our team's accomplishments included:

- Top battle-efficiency award
- Community-service awards
- Awards for retaining and taking care of people
- Outstanding ballistic-missile submarine in the Atlantic Fleet
- Navy's Meritorious Unit Commendation
- Top strategic-missile unit in the nation (competing with all of the Navy's strategic submarines and all U.S. Air Force strategic-missile units). In 1996 the *Nebraska* became the first *Ohio*-class submarine to win the prestigious Omaha Trophy award

for excellence. The *Nebraska* was lauded in particular for "a successful launch of two Trident II (D-5) test missiles for follow-on Commander in Chief Evaluation Testing."[30]

In 1999, while I commanded Submarine Squadron Four, one of the submarines in the squadron won the prestigious Battenberg Cup award for excellence, becoming the first submarine in this award's ninety-nine-year history to win. All Atlantic Fleet aircraft carriers, ships, and submarines already selected as top Battle Efficiency award-winners compete annually for the Battenberg.

Operation Enduring Freedom: The *Kitty Hawk* (CV-63) aircraft-carrier strike group (Carrier Group Five) demonstrated exceptional teamwork in 2001. They were instrumental during the initial combat strikes against adversaries in Afghanistan shortly after the 11 September 2001 (9/11) attacks on our nation.

In the year 2000, I had the opportunity to serve as chief of staff (second in command) of the ten-ship *Kitty Hawk* group. Carrier Strike Group Five is the U.S. Navy's only permanently forward-deployed strike group. Its homeport was in Yokosuka, Japan. Serving with two different strike-group commanders, I was able to learn quite a bit about joint, coalition, and fleet-wide operations. The operating pace was relatively high, as we conducted operations and engagement with our allies and partners for about 65 percent of this two-year assignment.

After 9/11, the *Kitty Hawk* strike group was assigned short-notice tasking to support the coalition efforts to counter the Taliban and other adversaries in Afghanistan. We got under way in late September 2001 from Yokosuka, at high speed to the Arabian Sea (one of the Seven Seas). I recalled the similar short-notice mission I had experienced in the *Louisville* ten years earlier. Now as chief of staff, I was able to work with the commander and the team to apply some of the lessons I had previously learned.

On 7 October 2001, on board the *Kitty Hawk*, we participated in the initial combat strikes of Operation Enduring Freedom against our enemies in Afghanistan. History records that the *Kitty Hawk* carrier strike-group mission was successful, as a preliminary coalition response to the 9/11 attacks.

The demonstrated teamwork and leadership was recognized as our strike group received the Navy Unit Commendation. The *Kitty Hawk* "superbly served as the Afloat Forward Staging Base (AFSB) for special operations combat forces and helicopters, garnering praise from the commanding general as 'the Best Ever AFSB.'"[31]

Cooperative Strategy for 21st Century Seapower: As a flag officer during 2002–10, my service included a tour as commander of Submarine Group 9, and then as director of global operations at U.S. Strategic Command. These were superb learning experiences for me as a leader.

In 2006, I was honored to become the sixth African American in the Navy's history to reach the rank of vice admiral, and the first African American submarine-qualified officer to reach three-star rank.

I was then privileged to serve as deputy commander of U.S. Fleet Forces Command, followed by assignment as commander of the U.S. Second Fleet. The Navy, Marine Corps, and Coast Guard applied our maritime strategy around the world effectively, because of the teamwork of dedicated people on the U.S. Fleet Forces Command Staff and U.S. Second Fleet Staff.

U.S. Second Fleet also contributes to homeland defense and is responsive to defense support to civil authorities after natural

In 2000, Captain Williams served on board the ten-ship *Kitty Hawk* (CV-63) Carrier Strike Group Five. As chief of staff, he was second in command of the Navy's only permanently forward-deployed strike group. After 9/11, they were assigned short-notice tasking to support efforts against the Taliban in Afghanistan. (U.S. Navy)

As commander of the U.S. Second Fleet (C2F), Vice Admiral Williams oversaw more than 90,000 sailors and Marines in a fleet of 130 ships and submarines, more than 1,500 aircraft, 4 carrier strike groups, 4 amphibious ready groups, 3 Marine expeditionary units, and Navy expeditionary combat command forces. Aside from homeland defense and responding to natural disasters such as the 2010 earthquake in Haiti, C2F contributed to combat efforts in Iraq and Afghanistan and helped to prevent war through forward presence and deterrence. Here, operations at sea in 2009. (U.S. Navy)

disasters such as 2008's Hurricane Ike in Galveston, Texas, and the 2010 earthquake in Haiti. Working with allies and partners, we contributed to the combat efforts in Iraq and Afghanistan as well as helping to prevent war through forward presence, deterrence, sea control, power projection, maritime security, and humanitarian assistance and disaster response.

One example of true commitment occurred during my tour as commander of the Second Fleet (C2F), when we responded to the devastating 7.0 earthquake in Haiti in January 2010. Because the staff, fleet senior leaders, sailors, and Marines assembled the best humanitarian-relief effort possible in a relatively short response time, we were able to provide rapid and effective support to the people of Haiti. C2F remains one of the Navy three-star joint task force–capable headquarters.

During this timeframe, C2F improved its operational level of war command and control capabilities, while C2F Maritime Operation Center daily execution also improved. We collaborated with the Coast Guard, the Canadian Navy, and other U.S. Navy fleets.

Among the team's accomplishments were safe and effective operations in a fleet of 130 ships and submarines, more than 1,500 aircraft, 4 carrier strike groups, 4 amphibious ready groups, 3 Marine expeditionary units, and Navy expeditionary combat command forces. More than 90,000 sailors and Marines were involved. Operations included a 23 percent fuel-expenditure reduction, resulting in energy conservation.

In July 2009, another country's submarines unexpectedly patrolled near U.S. East Coast waters. For the first time ever, selected Navy forces were shifted to U.S. Northern Command, and C2F conducted successful real-world Maritime Homeland Defense and Deterrence operations.

Because of probable global climate changes, the Arctic is now of increased strategic importance. The region is within the C2F area of responsibility, so we established an operational training plan with Canada and the U.S. Coast Guard to better prepare C2F forces for a potential supporting role in and near the Arctic.

In terms of providing ready maritime forces for global assignment, C2F trained and certified maritime forces that were then successful during combat operations supporting Central Command in Iraq and Afghanistan as well as operations in maritime security, counter piracy, and deterrence.

Our fleet irregular-warfare training was realistic, repeatable, and adaptive for independent deploying units. Counter-piracy training success was evident in April 2009, when shots from Navy SEALs on the USS *Bainbridge* (DDG-96) put into motion the rescue from Somali pirates of Captain Richard Phillips and the Maersk *Alabama*. Those shots were, of course, the result of five days of intensive and meticulously coordinated teamwork.

C2F also improved antisubmarine warfare training and expanded the use of fleet synthetic training as a means to maintain readiness while conserving energy. Regarding future force development, C2F led the certification for the USS *Freedom*'s (LCS-1) two-years-early deployment, as well as teaming with the Marine Corps' II Expeditionary Force to revitalize war fighting competency in amphibious operations. C2F earned the Golden Anchor Award for a high retention rate, developing leaders, and taking care of people.

Our efforts in terms of teaming with allies and partners to execute the maritime strategy included publishing the first NATO maritime counter-piracy tactics and providing to NATO the first maritime security operations concept. We worked with the NATO leadership to contribute to the Allied Maritime Strategy, the first for NATO in more than twenty years.

In all, my assignments were wonderful opportunities to serve and support thousands of sailors and Marines, and to support joint service, allies, partners, and coalition efforts in executing the U.S. Maritime Strategy. Our collective efforts were able to influence events not only in each of the Seven Seas, but globally.

Chapter Five

caring

Leadership includes caring and *serving needs*. Individual people, money, and time are all required to accomplish an objective, and the team as a whole has different requirements. The leader must remain aware of all of these and work diligently to obtain needed resources, while also having consideration of people's needs.

We believe that to care—that is, to have empathy, compassion, and consideration—is an essential aspect of effective leadership. It is a part of what makes us human. It acknowledges that we are each vulnerable to circumstances and that we are fallible. As Marcus Annaeus Seneca said, "Wherever there is a human being, there is an opportunity for a kindness."[32]

Caring is important. Leaders who care take action toward ***serving needs*** of their people. We believe that it is okay to have feelings. As a leader you can be strong and effective while also caring for others, as well as ensuring your own personal well-being. As we navigated, we found *caring* to be the ***fifth Leadership C***. Consider its key aspects:

- **self-knowledge and self-respect**
  Take care of your mind, body, and spirit. Continue to strive for balance in life. Endeavor to achieve peace of mind—be free of fear, resentment, anger, guilt, doubt, and worry.

- **faith**
  Spirituality is important. Faith provides strength.

- **family**
  Love your spouse and family. Have a few close friends who understand. Have relationships based on caring and trust.

- **people**
  Take care of your people. Serve their needs. Provide them with opportunity for personal and professional growth. Have consideration. Delegate authority (allowing for small mistakes). Align individual goals with organizational goals. Recognize accomplishment. Find out who is doing things right and thank them. Sincerity matters.

[Williams SR]

SELF, FAITH, FAMILY, PEOPLE

As I developed through the years, early on I had a good sense of ***self***. I tended to highlight my strengths, the Leadership Cs. I was self-confident, yet aware of my weaknesses and shortcomings.

My *faith* was strong and personal. I tried to live my faith in God through my actions and relationships with others. I have accepted what God granted me to have.

God saw to it that I was rewarded with a beautiful wife, Dora Ruth, who loved and respected me and who brought four wonderful children into our immediate ***family:*** Sharon, Veronica, Mel Jr., and Kenneth. Each child was special to us and is dearly loved. We accepted each one's offering to the world. For example, Kenneth was born with acute autism. He has never been verbal enough to communicate, and has been severely limited in many other ways. Ruth and I prayed for him to improve. I give Ruth all the credit for her faith and fortitude in finding a place for Kenneth in a group-home setting by the time he was twenty years old. Today he is properly cared for, and we frequently bring him home for visits.

Ruth Williams is a special person who has been by my side since 1953. She has supported me and our family with strength and love. I respect her views and her insights. She is a key reason for any success I may have realized during my career and beyond.

Ruth has not been unlike many spouses of military members, in that she cared for our family while I was away on deployments, including seeing to the daily needs of our kids, taking care of our home and our financial and social responsibilities. She is a strong and kind woman with wisdom.

Additionally, although she seldom talked about it, I knew she felt some internal discomfort in the 1960s and early 1970s, when she occasionally accompanied me to Navy social events at which we were the only African Americans. And sometimes my bosses invited Ruth and me to senior Navy officer events where we were the only enlisted couple. I remember times when she put on her "game face" and smiled, all the while being ignored by most of the other women present. It must have been a feeling of public loneliness. Even so, Ruth continued to attend the events to support me. I love her and thank her for who she is.

As Mel Jr. was growing up, it was clear to me that he was special. He made the usual errors of a young boy, but he listened, observed, and learned the right lessons from the right people. He knew that he wanted to pursue higher education and prepared himself accordingly. It was his decision to also pursue service via the Navy. Ruth and I supported his decision. We make it a point to maintain a ***strong family***.

Over the years Ruth and I have hosted family members at our home in the Washington, D.C., area. We have seen five generations of family members come through our home. We have always felt it to be important for the youngest to spend time with the elders. Hosting Williams and Pettes, particularly during the holiday periods, has been a wonderful experience. Despite the typical lifetime challenges that develop, we remain a strong African American family.

Of course, people cannot choose the families from which they come. Many leaders have overcome far from ideal personal circumstances and, through self-confidence and the other Leadership Cs, prevailed. Having a strong, loving family has been a bonus for which I will be eternally grateful. However, if you are not so fortunate, you can still become an effective and caring leader through ***developing relationships*** and ***creating your own extended family***. It is important to allow others into your personal life—to form connections and accept people fully, with both their strengths and their weaknesses.

From a leadership standpoint, I always tried to care for my people. I developed caring and trusting relationships. I tried to serve their needs and regularly recognized their accomplishments.

I truly believed that leaders must have consideration for the personal and professional needs of their people. Sincerity matters. There were countless times when I simply listened to the needs and desires of others, and took action to assist them. This was time-consuming, but necessary. As I reflect back, this care for others had an unexpected return on investment: trust and commitment to the team's efforts.

During my many years in the Navy, I found that service to others was important. Giving became a source of satisfaction and helped to make me a "whole" person, by which I mean someone who cares for others, helps others to succeed, and unselfishly supports the mission. I learned to do this from others with whom I worked, many of whom are named in the acknowledgments section of this book. I thank them all again.

[Williams JR]

To have empathy, consideration, and compassion is an essential aspect of effective leadership. ***Caring is part of what makes us human.*** It acknowledges that we are vulnerable to circumstances and fallible. ***Caring is linked to serving needs*** in our definition of leadership.

A caring and trusting relationship is critical for individuals to commit themselves in support of the leader, and also to establish the organizational cohesion necessary for a leader to create teamwork.

I join the ranks of many other senior leaders who understand the significance of genuinely caring for their people. It has been important for me to establish a human-to-human, caring and trusting relationship with the people I have both served and led.

In my experience, it is best that leaders establish such a relationship before asking individuals to do something for them or the team. And by the way, as noted previously, sincerity matters.

SELF

First and foremost, a leader must have ***self-knowledge***. Know who you are. Know your strengths and your weaknesses. Build on your strengths and improve your weak areas. Determine your purpose and passion.

With self-knowledge, you must then have ***self-respect***. This is a starting point for establishing relationships that are built on caring and trust.

I am a strong proponent of the Golden Rule: Do unto others as you would have them do unto you. The Bible notes this in several locations, both in the Jewish Bible/Christian Old Testament and in the New Testament:

"You shall not take vengeance or bear a grudge against any of your people, but you shall love your neighbor as yourself: I am the Lord" (Lev. 19:18, New Revised Standard Version).

"In everything do to others as you would have them do to you; for this is the law and the prophets" (Matt. 7:12, NRSV).

"Do to others as you would have them do to you" (Luke 6:31, NRSV).

Maintaining balance in your life is a part of self-respect. At times, this is easier said than done. When you are truly committed and dedicated to your purpose and passion, an imbalance can ensue if you do not attend to the other parts of your being and your life.

As a matter of self-respect, engage proactively in ***time management*** to ensure ***appropriate balance between mind, body, and spirit.***

Commitment and dedication to duty and work are important, but it is also critical that time be apportioned to develop your mind (read for pleasure, take time for self-improvement and quiet time to think and reflect), exercise your body, and be aware of your spirituality.

During my various assignments, staff have noted on my daily schedules "PT," for physical training. This is needed. They have also noted "executive time," which indicates fencing off my personal time to think and reflect. My long-range schedules have days allotted for time off and leave with family and friends.

These time-management actions (fenced-off personal time) have not been perfect, simply because unplanned events periodically occur on a day-to-day basis and necessitate my attention at the expense of time to myself. Nevertheless, this has been my approach.

For me, self-knowledge, self-respect, the Golden Rule, and maintaining balance have been entry points to self, as I have entered and maintained relationships founded on caring and trust. Ultimately, for self I continue to seek peace of mind. This means being free of fear, resentment, anger, guilt, doubt, and worry. It is an ongoing pursuit.

FAITH

Faith provides strength. It helps to give me courage as a human being.

Our family is of the Christian faith. We believe in God. Regardless of your own beliefs, spirituality is an important part of maintaining balance.

For me, faith also helps to achieve peace of mind, as well as guide me in caring and trusting relationships. Franklin Delano Roosevelt held similar views: "The only limit to our realization of tomorrow will be our doubts of today. Let us move forward with strong and active faith."[33]

FAMILY

In his section previous to this one, my father noted that everyone is not fortunate enough to come from a strong family. But as he said, even if that is the case, it is important to create your own close circle of mutual support—this is a family.

Families help to keep us grounded in reality. They know us best. ***Families care.*** They give love that is needed as we deal with daily challenges. They support us and provide needed guidance and feedback. Accordingly, it is clearly essential to ***love and care for one's spouse and/or family.***

Melvin G. Williams Sr. and Dora Ruth Williams continue to be caring parents. They were key influencers of my character, as stated previously. My father set the example of how to be a loving father and servant leader. Although he spent the first fourteen of his twenty-seven-year career on sea duty (much of the time away from home on ships and submarines, serving in defense of freedom), he taught me many of life's lessons and imparted the right values. When home, he coached our little-league baseball and football games. He helped me with Boy Scouts and other activities. My father emphasized the importance of education and helped to ensure that I performed to my potential.

And, as described earlier, he helped me to gain entry to the U.S. Naval Academy Preparatory School. As a retired master chief, my father continues to provide me with counsel and feedback as the Navy addresses the challenges of today and tomorrow.

My mother, Ruth Williams, continues to be of quiet strength in the family. She raised four children and cared for us, providing love, discipline when needed, and the right values.

BEST WISHES

Our mother emphasized education and kept us in character-building activities. She led my Cub Scouts group and supported the many activities that helped us all to develop. Mom kept us clothed and fed, which was sometimes challenging in the 1960s on my father's modest pay of a junior petty officer. She obtained outside-the-home employment over the years, and went back to school for an associate's degree. My mother is special and remains a strong supporter of the U.S. Navy.

I met Donna Ree Williams, my spouse of more than thirty years, as we attended the same high-school algebra class in Suitland, Maryland. She did better than I. We did not date until our junior year. I played sports, and Donna was in the band. At graduation, we both walked across the stage as members of the National Honor Society.

We continued to date as she attended and graduated from the University of Maryland, while I attended and graduated from the Naval Academy. We were the first college graduates in our respective families. We married in 1978; one year later, Melvin G. Williams III was born.

Donna prefers that I not make mention of her caring contributions to me and the families at my commands, but you must know that she is a quiet, strong, loving person of the highest integrity. She is a big part of the modest success that our family has thus far enjoyed. Donna is a Navy spouse and mother who volunteers her time in support of my activities—while also raising our family and working in the accounting field for our first twenty years.

Melvin G. Williams III and Trinity Marie Williams are both caring children of whom we are proud parents.

Today in the U.S. Navy, more than 60 percent of service members are married. This is a much larger proportion relative to my

In this 2002 photo, Captain Williams (left) had recently been selected to the rank of rear admiral (lower half) and was traveling during free time with wife Donna and their children, Trinity and Mel III. (Courtesy of the authors)

father's Navy generation. We have been an all-volunteer armed force since 1972.

Caring for the families of employees is important. They are a vital extension of the employee. Leaders, whether in the armed forces or in public or private industry, should give due regard to the care of families of those who work in their organizations.

Families count when it comes to an employee's commitment and willingness to enter caring and trusting relationships at work.

It is also important for leaders to have a few good friends whom they can truly trust. For me, Gary McCorkle and his family have been friends since childhood. The U.S. Naval Academy Class of 1978 continues to provide me with good friends who care, understand, and are supportive. Former and current shipmates are included in my network of good friends.

PEOPLE

There is no question that ***leaders must take care of their people.*** People must know that leaders care, and leaders must take action toward ***serving the needs*** of their people.

Technology, systems, and processes are important for management and efficiency, but people are the key to effectiveness.

Taking care of people includes providing them with ***opportunities*** for personal and professional growth and development. It means delegating to them the authorities that enable growth—even if small mistakes are made. It involves aligning the goals for each individual with the organizational goals. This is a win-win situation.

Taking care of your people includes ***treating them with dignity and respect*** and ***serving needs.*** It means providing them with the resources necessary to be successful as they do their jobs and develop.

When you take care of your people, you ***recognize accomplishments***—not just annual awards of with bonuses, but also with on-the-spot acknowledgement of a job well done.

And you develop relationships based on caring and trust. ***Basic human kindness is contagious.***

I continue to strive toward improving my ability to serve as a leader of people. This requires a significant investment in time, but the investment is in doing what is right. As Chinese philosopher Lao Tzu wrote hundreds of years before the birth of Christ:

> Kindness in words creates confidence.
> Kindness in thinking creates profoundness.
> Kindness in giving creates love.[34]

A DAY IN THE OFFICE: 5 JANUARY 2009

This was the first day back at the office after a holiday period. It was a relatively light workday, started by using my treadmill at home and saying my morning prayer. At the office, I was greeted by Yeoman Chief Eric Nelson, a loyal and caring leader. We have served together for nearly eight years in four different assignments.

I then participated in a morning staff alignment meeting. The chief of staff noted that a chief petty officer (CPO) had allegedly abused his government credit card by charging personal items, which is not permitted. Initially the staff planned to conduct an investigation, which could have led to formal charges and career-ending punishment.

My guidance to the chief of staff and fleet command master chief was that one of them should meet with the suspected CPO to ascertain any obvious root causes or personal issues. The question was: Why would a twenty-one-year CPO commit such an offense?

The fleet command master chief did meet with the CPO, who, it turned out, was having marital problems and had overextended himself financially. He admitted guilt, was counseled, and paid the unauthorized charges. Our command leadership agreed to help this twenty-one-year veteran resolve his issues without the adverse effects of career-ending punishment.

After the morning staff meeting that launched this process, I took care of correspondence. I wrote a note to a junior officer former shipmate to wish him and his family a happy new year, responding to a Christmas card he had sent our family. I also wrote to an officer whom I mentor, congratulating him on his selection to receive a nationally recognized professional award for career achievement. In a letter of recommendation to the Navy's promotion selection board, I strongly endorsed another staff member for selection for promotion. Finally, I signed a promotion recommendation for a staff U.S. Air Force officer, after asking a two-star Air Force officer friend of mine to review his record.

Moving on to other activities, a one-star admiral reported for duty to our command for duty, so we presented him with a personal letter welcoming him and his family. Next, I met with Chief Nelson to schedule engagements for visiting sailors and Marines. We had recently visited six countries and thirty-two ships, submarines, and aviation units.

By now it was lunchtime. After that I traveled to the office of another one-star admiral to say hello and give him the opportunity to update me on his initiatives. I invited him and his command master chief to visit any of our ships to help them with their plans.

With yet another one-star admiral, I then discussed an operational decision. He had to make a determination as to whether or not to get his ships under way in view of the inclement weather conditions. I listened, then told him that I trusted his judgment.

Next it was time to meet with staff and listen to recommendations about whether or not to change a ship's schedule on the day of a planned operation. I made an unpopular decision and communicated it to staff, my boss, and four other admirals.

An intelligence briefing was next. I directed operational action to address the situation, and complimented the junior officer who presented the briefing. Finally I received an operational update briefing and provided commander's guidance. I thanked the team for the briefing.

At the end of that day in the office, I gratefully arrived home to greet my wife and daughter. Our son was already grown and living on his own in the Washington D.C. area.

In America, "Eternal Father" is often called the "Navy Hymn" because it is sung at the Naval Academy. It is also sung on ships of the British Royal Navy and has been translated into French. This was the favorite hymn of U.S. President Franklin Roosevelt and was sung at his funeral in Hyde Park, New York, 15 April 1945. The Navy Band played it on 25 November 1963 as U.S. President John Kennedy's body was carried up the steps of the U.S. Capitol to lie in state. Roosevelt served as Secretary of the Navy, and Kennedy was a patrol-boat commander in World War II.

Eternal Father, strong to save,
Whose arm hath bound the restless wave,
Who biddest the mighty ocean deep
Its own appointed limits keep;
Oh, hear us when we cry to Thee,
For those in peril on the sea!
O Christ! Whose voice the waters heard

And hushed their raging at Thy Word,
Who walked on the foaming deep,
And calm amidst its rage didst sleep;
Oh, hear us when we cry to Thee,
For those in peril on the sea!
Most Holy Spirit! Who didst brood
Upon the chaos dark and rude,
And bid its angry tumult cease,
And give, for wild confusion, peace;
Oh, hear us when we cry to Thee,
For those in peril on the sea!
O Trinity of love and power!
Our family shield in danger's hour;
From rock and tempest, fire and foe,
Protect us wheresoever we go;
Thus evermore shall rise to Thee
Glad hymns of praise from land and sea.

Chapter Six

communicating

Inspiring action is accomplished through communicating. People want to be inspired by the leader, who provides a sense of purpose and a reason for commitment to the team's effort. However, an inspirational speech without a plan, and without the right and timely action, may prove to be labor lost. The leader needs to develop forward-looking plans with the team, and take action while creating a sense of urgency. Leaders must assess progress (that is, they must measure and see for themselves), adjust, adapt, and execute.

Abraham Lincoln said: "Extemporaneous speaking should be practiced and cultivated. It is the lawyer's avenue to the public. However able and faithful he may be in other respects, people are slow to bring him business if he cannot make a speech."[35]

Communicating is important. Leaders must be effective in inspiring action. Both of us had to work hard to improve our ability to communicate. And although today we are clearly not the best in this area, we have found that leaders must be effective communicators.

Accordingly, we found ***communicating*** to be the ***sixth Leadership C*** as we navigated. Its key aspects are:

- **listening**
  It is best to listen much more than you speak.

- **transmitting**
  A leader must be able to communicate effectively in writing and when speaking. Master the art of extemporaneous speaking. Be clear. Be brief.

- **achieving understanding**
  Communicate to achieve understanding. Understanding often leads to commitment and action. Endeavor to find and remove barriers to effective communication.

- **inspiring**
  As a leader, seek to inspire people toward desired action. Foster teamwork, as organizational cohesion is absolutely essential. Provide hope.

[Williams SR]

LISTENING, TRANSMITTING, ACHIEVING UNDERSTANDING, INSPIRING

Listening and understanding may certainly lead to cooperation. I purposefully elected to go back to sea duty as my final assignment in the Navy. After years in the Pentagon, and after initiating change to an enlisted rating, I wanted to lead the effectiveness of that change at sea.

When I accepted the job as command master chief of the *Piedmont* I was forty-three years old, while the average age of the crew was about nineteen. This is the standard generational communications challenge that senior leaders face.

One of the issues I endeavored to address on board the ship was that too many young sailors were getting into trouble and appearing at captain's mast for adjudication of discipline infractions. The *Piedmont* had a basketball team with a good following among the crew. I decided to attend one of the games. I did not say anything at the game, but I did cheer for the team. The crew knew I was present and was apprehensive about approaching "the old chief."

I started attending each game and invited a senior shipmate, James Mullin (later to become a command master chief). Soon we were cheering together. By attending the games and quietly providing support, I was able to determine who the informal leader was among the young sailors. I took the opportunity to talk to him about efforts to reduce discipline infractions and trips to see the old man, or captain's mast.

Over time, understanding was achieved. Eventually we reduced the captain's mast list to zero. When there was a discipline infraction, the individual was invited to my stateroom to deal with me. If appropriate, the offender also had to apologize to shipmates.

The captain asked me, "What are you feeding the crew?" He was astonished at the behavior change. But it occurred ***without much transmitting*** or preaching. We ***achieved understanding***.

In my heart, I always loved the stewards. They were top-notch sailors who were dedicated and generally not given the positive recognition they deserved. In 1995, seventeen years after my retirement from the Navy, the Units K-West and B-East U.S. Navy Mess Attendants Association asked me to be a keynote speaker. This veterans' group is named for the barracks locations that, starting in 1932, were assigned to stewards at school in Norfolk, Virginia.

I began my remarks by noting: "I am not a seasoned public speaker. I should be sitting out there with you, relaxing, nursing a cool one, and smoking a cigar." This put us all on the same level and broke the ice.

From there I moved on my intent for the evening, which was simply to recognize what these people could do and what they could still accomplish. "There is scripture in the Bible found in Proverbs that says, 'whoso keepeth his mouth and his tongue, keepeth his soul from troubles.' There will be no speech tonight, however I will attempt to tell you a story."

I am told that it was ***inspirational***. I spoke of the unacknowledged, yet sincerely dedicated, service and sacrifice of thousands of messmen and stewards who simply did their jobs in support of our nation; and of the faceless sailors who tried to make a positive difference for their shipmates, their families, and themselves during a period in our country when opportunities for minorities were quite limited.

My story was about the quiet determination and professionalism of sailors who overcame obstacles and persevered to help the Navy achieve an institutional change in culture, leading to acceptance of all people for who they are. It was about how messmen's and stewards' unheralded actions resulted in the development of opportunities for future generations—as in the case of my son, Vice Admiral Mel Williams Jr.

That keynote address was followed by other occasions on which I and others, including the writer Richard Miller, began communicating the story of the unsung efforts of former dedicated Navy stewards. Miller's book, *The Messman's Chronicles*, was published in November 2003 (Naval Institute Press).

A retired Navy chief hospital corpsman, Miller, in this major study, covers the widespread and long-enduring discrimination against those of non-white races. He, several others, and I have proactively sought appropriate recognition for former stewards. As detailed earlier, these efforts included our push to name a Navy destroyer in honor of William Pinckney, who earned the Navy Cross during World War II. Other tributes toward which we worked include a historical marker at the site of the former barracks K-West and B-East at the Norfolk Navy Base, and another historical marker at the stewards' area on board the ex-USS *North Carolina* (BB-55) in Wilmington, North Carolina.

One of our efforts included an event in September 2008 at the Naval Academy. Congressman Elijah Cummings joined the Academy's superintendent, the brigade of midshipmen, and an assembly of more than 200 former Navy stewards to dedicate a historical marker in the King Hall mess at Bancroft Hall. The plaque commemorates the former stewards who served and supported midshipmen over the years. This was a glorious event that Ruth attended, along with our daughters, Mel Jr., and Donna.

The former stewards' service and efforts will, hopefully, inspire current and future sailors to strive for excellence in the service of our nation.

Before my 1978 retirement, I returned to sea duty for my final tour, as I've mentioned. As a contributor to the *Navy Supply Corps Newsletter*, I felt that it was important to communicate my perspective on the mess-management specialist rating, especially after

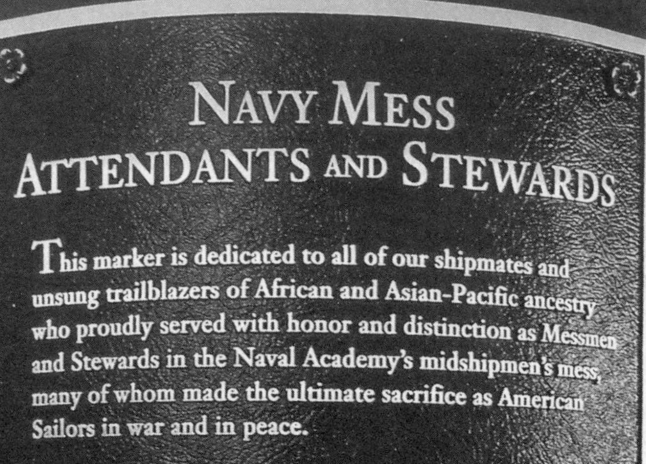

Among the historical markers placed by Master Chief Williams's Navy Mess Attendants Association is this one, placed in 2008 to commemorate the messmen and stewards who served in the U.S. Naval Academy mess, King Hall. (U.S. Navy)

having worked so hard toward its implementation. Because this article summarized the problems and reviewed the overall situation, I offer it here in its entirety. It was printed in the July 1976 issue.

The Merger: What Does It Mean?

A Mess Management Specialist Perspective
By MSCM Melvin G. Williams

It has been better than one year since the Commissaryman (CS) and Stewards (SD) communities were merged to form the Navy's newest rating: Mess Management Specialist (MS). An immediate result was that under manning was alleviated in the CS community and over manning no longer existed in the SD community. Since the merger, changes have taken place which when employed have given the MS rating greater diversity, increased responsibility, and a better professional image.

Within the areas of greater diversity the new dimensions of learning the job of your new counterparts and retraining are foremost. These new job skills, if retained and practiced, allow for not only greater flexibility in our rating but also the development of more marketable skills for future use within the civilian hospitality field at the end of our naval careers. Gourmet cooking, napkin folding, vegetable carving, garnishing, formal service, and special meals (i.e., birthday month, captain's night, etc.) are important knowledge factors to acquire and employ. Our rating is expanding with the addition of BEQ management and to a lesser degree club management, which have been included in our billet structure. When interfaced with our food service capabilities, these additions give the MS rating a well-rounded career pattern.

Both Williamses attended the King Hall historical-plaque ceremony, here with Superintendent Vice Admiral Jeffrey L. Fowler. (U.S. Naval Academy)

Increased responsibility goes hand in glove with promotions. With the merger, the MS rating has been fortunate in the area of promotion opportunities. Paygrades E-4 through E-9 have proportionately and in many cases numerically exceeded most ratings in the Navy, awarding both the 3501 (SD) and the 3502 (CS) communities. It is interesting to note that the 3501 sector has received high numbers of promotions in the E-4/E-5 paygrades, while the 3502 sector has received increased numbers in the E-8/E-9 paygrades. These promotions provide the opportunity for younger personnel to be involved with all phases of responsibilities, thus creating the avenue for new and fresh initiatives.

Historically, if we allow ourselves to be truthful, food service personnel have not been looked upon with the same esteem as have some ratings in the Navy. The old stereotyped "stew burner" image was cast upon us. Perhaps in the old days when the "Bill of Fare" on naval vessels consisted of salt horse, plum duff, and cracker hash, our image was molded. Throughout the years we have continued to refine our skills. Gone are stew burners, replaced by the best of two worlds concept (CS/SD), for providing fast, efficient, and courteous service to our customers. The initiatives employed by the Navy Food Service Teams, the NEY awards competition, the service schools; joined by the Steward instruction and demonstration teams, the Navy messes and club awards, and the E. R. Zumwalt awards for BEQs, give our new rating a greater sense of respectability and image. We have all arrived at this point together, where we can provide formal meals or mass feeding, shipboard or ashore meals, and club or BEQ management.

There are some areas within the rating that we in the community have to strengthen if we desire to have a viable dynamic rating for the future. Among the areas that need concerted effort are cross training and recruiting.

Cross training is essential for the successful implementation of this merger. To look for excuses not to move forward Navy-wide toward this commitment would case undue constraints on future operations of our rating. Due to the time schedule as outlined in the milestones for full qualification for all hands by 1978, it would seem that we should be further ahead than we are. It is reported that some commands are making the transition while others are having difficulties. With these ideas in mind, it would seem: (1) that each command should be required to make a progress report to NAVSUP, at least biannually, in this area for the sake of uniformity during this transitional training period and (2) that it be mandatory that each command that has not started the rotational pools do so, to assist in the cross training.

In addition to the efforts made on the mess decks and rotational pools to non-rated personnel with potential to consider the MS rating, the Recruiting Command should be provided literature depicting the scope and importance of the MS rating and its direct relationship to mission accomplishment. Such an overview, once edited and disseminated, would serve well the person sincerely interested in the food service and hospitality field. It should be noted that ample recruiting is necessary to sustain present and future manning requirements of this newly formed community.

In my view, the merger has given the impetus for greater depth in the MS career pattern, broadened advancement and training opportunities and the chance to stay abreast of private industry. Presently opportunities within the MS rating are unlimited, however, we must continue to ensure that sound management practices and training expertise are provided throughout the Mess Management Specialist rating if we are to maintain our present success.

[Williams JR]

Leaders must be effective in communicating to inspire action. Effective communication leads to understanding, commitment, and action toward desired effectiveness.

I have had to work hard to improve my communication skills. It became clear to me early on that effective communications were essential for people to achieve understanding of the subject matter. When people understood, including the reasons for something or the intended results or effects, they were more inclined to commit to taking action.

It also became clear that it was important to ***keep people informed.*** Followers must be kept apprised of the status as a means of synchronizing individual actions, and to let them know they are part of a unified effort.

LISTENING

It is my view that a leader should listen more than transmit. ***You cannot learn while you are transmitting.***

I work to remain quiet during meetings and visits with our people. During private, one-on-one meetings, I sometimes chew on my unlighted pipe to help me refrain from speaking.

A periodic, non-threatening but purposeful question in conversations has helped me to keep others transmitting while I listen and learn. Sometimes people have not been familiar with me, or have been uncomfortable because seniority can get in the way of openness. In such cases I have transmitted as appropriate to establish a caring and trusting relationship. This has generally involved finding some human condition or event that we might have in common.

Listening requires patience. Accordingly, the more senior I became (with, perhaps, more knowledge and experience than most of my people), the more patience I had to develop to allow others to communicate their views. Patience takes effort, particularly with the time constraints that a leader has.

I found it counterproductive to interrupt someone's transmission or come back immediately with a counterpoint. But I had to work at not doing this, keeping in mind that the interlocutor knows that interruptions or immediate retorts require formulation of thought—which occurs while the leader should be listening. Body language, eye contact, and an occasional acknowledgment constitute a listener's tool set.

One of the most important aspects of listening is the leader's ***follow-up action.*** After paying attention and learning from my people, I have found it critical to take visible and tangible action on noteworthy inputs, as appropriate according to the situation. Those who provide input must know that their ideas were made actionable. After the listening session, my practice has been to publicly communicate appreciation for the inputs when possible.

TRANSMITTING AND ACHIEVING UNDERSTANDING

My efforts continue toward improving my ability to ***write, speak, and communicate nonverbally.*** I have tried to keep my transmissions short and to the point. ***Be clear. Be brief.*** Too much written or verbal interaction results in overload for subordinates and in many situations inhibits their understanding. It takes much effort to condense complex subjects into concise messages that can be understood. Seek help from public-affairs experts and from the deck plates, your audience base, as appropriate. In general, when possible your communications message should be not only clear and brief, but also in some way linked to the leader's vision and desired effectiveness.

My people would tell you that I can sometimes sound like a broken record (or a defective CD), in that I tend to ***continually reaffirm the vision, goals, and focus areas of the organization.*** I do try to vary the way in which I do this—and the intended consequence has been that most people know the vision, goals, and focus areas of the organization.

When transmitting the communications message, it is important to periodically ***provide strategic context.*** People need to know why what they are being asked to do is important, and how it links to the bigger picture. ***Visualizations*** can be an effective way to convey how a junior person's lower-level action contributes to the larger, greater-than-self effort. Creating a visual image and using language and stories that resonate with the people are helpful tools to achieve understanding.

I have learned to embrace ***extemporaneous speaking.*** The following anecdote illustrates how useful this can be.

A senior petty officer was in charge of our command's mentoring program with a local elementary school in North Florida. One day while I was in port, he invited me to visit the school. This was not on my agenda for that day, but it was described to me as an impromptu way to allow young students to engage with the commander. I agreed. My expectation, as we traveled there, was that I would meet the teachers and students one on one, and also visit classrooms during session. Upon arrival, the principal greeted me and escorted me to the auditorium.

I entered and found myself in the opening scene of the movie *Patton.* Hundreds of students and teachers quietly sat or stood in the audience, while I was on an elevated stage with a single microphone on a pole in the center. An oversized American flag covered the wall behind the stage. Immediately I was directed to the microphone, while the principal announced: "Students and faculty, our guest speaker today is Commander Mel Williams Jr."

It happened to be Flag Day! Unlike those of General George S. Patton, my extemporaneous remarks were delivered in clean language, appropriate for the young. But similarly to Patton, they were brief and to the point.

I said, "Greetings everyone! I am pleased to be with you today as we honor the flag of our great nation. Regardless of our backgrounds, or whether you are a boy named Tom or a girl named Sue, as Americans we must continue to respect the colors of our national flag—red, white and blue."

My talk was well received. The lesson I learned was to embrace and be ready for extemporaneous speaking opportunities at any time.

Over the years, I have tried to communicate by employing ***as many means and methods as possible***. I have sent a consistent message verbally and in writing, backed up nonverbally by as many twenty-first-century methods as have been appropriate. Many leaders today are benefiting from the Internet and social networking to communicate with customers and potential employees.

It is essential to ***find and remove physical and psychological barriers to effective communication***. Typical barriers include the following.

- The "human engineering" of an operational space or office may not be conducive to sharing information and communicating.

- The communications path may be vertical instead of horizontal. The problem with this is that if a barrier arises in the vertical path, it can never be surpassed so that the information can reach the lowest levels of the organization. Horizontal communications avoid the barrier in the first place.
- The entire scope, breath, and reach of the message may not be conveyed, although needed. To overcome this barrier, ***reach out to several audiences***, as appropriate. Families should be considered. The U.S. Navy employs command ombudsmen, generally the spouse of a service member, to facilitate two-way communications between the commander and families.
- Lack of ***commitment*** and negative ***attitudes*** can inhibit effective communication. This is a leader's challenge to address. It helps to develop relationships based on caring and trust.

Feedback must be obtained to assess whether understanding of the message has been achieved. ***The communications process is not complete until the receiver receives and understands.*** Listening to people during visits is one way to get feedback. Another is to listen to the equivalent of your master chief petty officer (senior enlisted) at your organization. You can also obtain feedback using any number of twenty-first-century technologies. And, most importantly, you can generate it when you assess the achievement of desired effectiveness—including on the levels of morale, commitment, and performance.

INSPIRING

People want to be inspired by a leader. They desire a feeling of purpose. This is not so much about cheerleading as it is about the leader's responsibility to ***see and be seen***, be ***forward-looking*** (have vision) and ***positive***, and provide ***hope***.

People want to be inspired by a leader, who needs to develop forward-looking plans with the team and take action while creating a sense of urgency. A routine, yet critical part of Vice Admiral Williams's job was to communicate effectively with and inspire senior commanders, staff, and crew (here in an aircraft carrier). (U.S. Navy)

The leader's inspiration helps ignite people to motivate themselves toward self-development and a commitment to take action to achieve the organization's desired effectiveness and vision.

Inspiration is essential to the creation of teamwork, which has been previously discussed. The following anonymous quote resonates with me:

> Hope works in these ways: it looks for the good in people instead of harping on the worst; it discovers what can be done instead of grumbling about what cannot; it regards problems, large and small, as opportunities; it pushes ahead when it would be easy to quit; it "lights the candle" instead of "cursing the darkness."[36]

As a leader, it is inspirational to me to know about and appreciate the many contributions of those who have served before me in defense of freedom. My father and the dedicated, professional sailors who served in the Navy before me helped to create opportunities of which we who have since volunteered to serve are the beneficiaries. We stand on their shoulders.

As I walked out the front door of my three-star-admiral headquarters in Norfolk, Virginia, I was inspired by the historical marker across the street. It designates the location of the former Navy school in which minorities were trained to be messmen and stewards. Pictured earlier in this book, the plaque reads:

> **Navy Mess Attendant School**
>
> From 1933 to 1942, Navy recruits of African descent attended this school, located in barracks at Unit "K-West" and later at "B-East." Advancement opportunities for these sailors and

> counterparts of Asian-Pacific island heritage were then limited to serving as officer's cooks or stewards. The school moved to Unit "X" in 1942 before training was relocated to Bainbridge, Maryland, and elsewhere. Though racial segregation continued, all job ratings were re-opened to qualified personnel in 1942. Mess attendants were re-designated "steward's mates" in 1943, and more than 1,100 members of the messman/steward branch were killed during World War II. Norfolk trainees decorated for heroism include Navy Cross recipients Doris Miller, William Pinckney, and Leonard Harmon.

It is an inspiration to me to watch as service members and their families continue to serve, sacrifice, and support the defense of freedom—in combat and in the prevention of war. It has been my privilege to serve and to lead.

Vice Admiral Williams leads Commander, U.S. Second Fleet senior staff at a change-of-flagship ceremony in 2009, with the USS *Bataan* (LHD-5) and USS *Iwo Jima* (LHD-7). (U.S. Navy)

The USS *Samuel Gravely* (DDG-107) was christened in May 2009 in honor of the first African American to reach the rank of flag officer, eventually as vice admiral. In attendance at the commissioning ceremony were (from left): Admiral (retired) J. Paul Reason, the first African American to reach four-star rank; Diane Reason; Mike Petters, corporate vice president and president of Northrop Grumman Shipbuilding; Alma Gravely; the Hon. B. J. Penn, first African American Acting Secretary of the Navy; Loretta Penn; Vice Admiral Williams; and Commander Douglas Kunzman, CO of the ship. (U.S. Navy)

In a habit picked up from Williams Sr. (here in 1964), Williams Jr. began early in his career chewing on an unlighted pipe to help him refrain from making decisions that a lesser experienced person would make. This leadership tool facilitated their professional development and growth. (Courtesy of the authors)

CELEBRATING COMMITMENT TO HONOR, DUTY AND COUNTRY

USBE INFORMATION TECHNOLOGY

US BLACK ENGINEER

THE BLACK COMMUNITY'S TECHNOLOGY MAGAZINE

$6.95

2007's MOST IMPORTANT BLACKS IN TECHNOLOGY LIST

Vice Admiral
Melvin G. "Mel" Williams, Jr.
U.S. Fleet Forces Command
Deputy Commander

THE TOP BLACKS IN THE MILITARY

http://www.blackengineer.com

Professional affinity groups and the deliberate recognition of achievements can be extremely beneficial for leaders who are developing their skills. In 2007, Vice Admiral Williams was noted among many senior leaders as one of the top blacks in the military. *U.S. Black Engineer Information Technology* is published by Career Communications Group, whose president and CEO, Dr. Tyrone Taborn, also sponsors the annual Black Engineer of the Year Awards. (USBE Information Technology)

Chapter Seven

community

Leadership involves regard for community when *creating teamwork*. With individuals who are better prepared and developed, the leader must work to create a cohesive team, so that the whole team is greater than the sum of the individuals. Cooperation is vital.

Dr. Martin Luther King Jr. said:

> The most creative turn of events in man's long history occurred when man set down his stone ax and began to cooperate with his neighbor. That seemingly elementary decision set in motion what we know now as civilization.
>
> At the heart of all civilization has meant and developed is "community"—the mutually cooperative and voluntary venture of man to assume a semblance of responsibility for his brother.[37]

Each of us is different, and this may present to some leaders many challenges in achieving the unity of effort to accomplish a task. However, we believe that individual differences make an organization stronger and provide the leader with additional opportunities toward improving organizational effectiveness, particularly when the leader values diversity of background, experience, culture, and thought.

Community is important. Leaders should endeavor to establish community strength when creating teamwork. Both of us have worked to apportion time for giving back and supporting others. Therefore, as we navigated, we acknowledged ***community*** as the ***seventh Leadership C***. Consider its key aspects:

- **diversity**
  Value our diversity. Honor differences. Seek to understand others who are of different backgrounds, experiences, cultures, and thoughts. When creating teamwork, diversity helps to make the organization as strong as a close community, as well as more effective.

- **mentoring**
  Share the wisdom that you have acquired.

- **assimilating**
  Learn to be comfortable with people who are different than you. Interact professionally and socially with people from different backgrounds and cultures. Seek and achieve cooperation.

- **youth**
  Give back to our youth. They are the legacy of our efforts as adults.

[Williams SR]

DIVERSITY

It is preferable to create "community strength" teamwork to achieve effectiveness and vision. Our diversity should be integral to our efforts to build a community and a team. It makes us stronger. I know this from personal experience, as illustrated in an example from 1956, when diversity was not in vogue.

That year I was assigned on board a destroyer tender ship, the *Prairie*. We were conducting a world cruise to demonstrate the U.S. Navy's forward presence and deterrence capabilities. Egypt had blocked the Suez Canal, thus the ship had to transit around the southern tip of Africa.

We stopped at Capetown, South Africa, which at the time observed apartheid as a matter of policy. South Africa recognized three categories of people: Caucasian (of European descent), colored (any non-white person), and native (of African descent).

Before our scheduled liberty port visit in Capetown, the commanding officer required everyone on the ship to identify themselves by race and ethnicity. This caused problems, as we had crew members of Mexican, Filipino, Hawaiian, and Japanese descent who did not identify with any of the three racial categories. In particular, they did not consider themselves to be "colored."

To be allowed to go ashore, we all had to agree not to violate any of the local laws. Anyone who was not of European background was declared "colored." Many individuals refused to go ashore. But the African Americans did not find things too different from what we had been experiencing in our own country at the time.

For many of us, important lessons were learned about the pervasiveness and injustice of racism. I did my best, while in the Navy, to help bring about change.

While I was assigned at the Pentagon in 1970 as a senior chief petty officer, one of the few African Americans assigned to duty there, I wrote the following letter regarding persistent racial discrimination.

22 May 1970
Dear Sir:

As a member of the United States Navy with more than 18 years of military service, I feel I must give my personal suggestions for promoting harmonious relationships between the various races within the armed forces.

It is now evident that the present problems now being experienced within the military services are mainly carry-overs from difficulties and experiences taking place "outside the gate" in civilian life. With these factors in mind, we must place emphasis on off-duty hours both within the military compounds and in the neighboring communities surrounding military establishments. There is a definite imbalance between what goes on outside the gate and what happens inside, which when paralleled is never ending. It goes without saying that military men cannot legislate or order civilian businessmen to welcome all people to their particular business establishments, but changes can come in an owner's attitude as a result of the proper attitudes among the main body of the military personnel patronizing these establishments. Therefore a strong indoctrination program should be implemented by the military to its own personnel [regarding] personal responsibilities and attitudes.

Each command could form a multiracial unit or morale team consisting of senior enlisted personnel working along with certain key younger enlisted personnel. This particular unit should be composed of volunteers with special qualities in human relations, the "guys who get along" type; commands should encourage participation. During the off-duty hours some of these people should be seen at the bowling alleys, roller rinks, base enlisted clubs, and other places the men frequent in order to get the feel and to encourage proper attitudes whenever situations might occur. In addition to this aspect they should serve as counselors and advisors during the working day, in the barracks, the mess halls, and other key meeting places. As representatives of the C.O. they should be able to make recommendations to the command as to changes in needs, desires, and priorities of the men in any given locale.

As far as the military is concerned there is a need to pay particular attention to the problem areas *now* and examine the causes for the problems. A prime spot on which to focus attention is Okinawa. This is an area where racism is prevalent on all fronts, where groups are locked together by races, where cliques are formed, and where racial separatism is the rule. These situations are for the betterment of no one. This separatism trend is evident on many overseas bases, as a result of years of neglect of the desires of personnel needs during off-duty hours. Here at home we know the reasons. These things should be corrected as soon as possible.

> One other possible suggestion would be to set up a multiracial staff built around the senior enlisted man in each service, with each man in the staff having a title and proper publicity. These men would tour various areas and try to instill leadership and pride through the achievement method.
>
> As a black military man I know that pride and respect through the ranks, up and down, a thing surely lacking in the past, can do much among the troops of color. For the Caucasian and black together, proper, "up-to-date" indoctrination will surely be a step in the right direction, with this growing problem.
>
> Very respectfully,
> Melvin G. Williams, SDC, USN
> SECNAV-CNO FLAG MESS
> RM 4D656 Pentagon
> Washington, D.C. 20350

One of the issues that Chief of Naval Operations Admiral Zumwalt had to address was the considerable racial unrest in the Navy—and the nation—in the early 1970s. Few minorities or women held high leadership positions. I perceived a lack of understanding about the needs and concerns of these populations, as well as a lack of opportunity for upward mobility in the Navy.

Tensions escalated, with significant unrest and turmoil on some Navy ships in 1972, including the aircraft carriers *Kitty Hawk* and *Constellation* (CVA-64) and the fuel-replenishment ship USS *Hassayampa* (T-AO-145). This had a major adverse effect on the ships' mission readiness and effectiveness.

Admiral Zumwalt led a number of sweeping reforms to address the situation, including groundbreaking policies that provided equal opportunity, enhanced understanding, and better care for families.

Today, though much remains to be done, Navy leaders value diversity and are working toward continued improvement. Men and women of all backgrounds and cultures now have opportunity to realize their full potential.

I can point with great pride and happiness to two personal examples that illustrate this point: First, thirty years after the *Kitty Hawk*'s racial unrest, Mel Jr. served as chief of staff (second in command) of the *Kitty Hawk* battle group. Knoblock wrote of the second illustration:

> As father Master Chief (Retired) Melvin Williams recalls after spending a day on USS *Nebraska* (Mel Jr.'s command), "I had lunch in the wardroom and reflected on many thoughts as I was served my meal. . . . I looked up at the Mess Management Specialist who was serving my food and saw that he was a white American. I looked up to the head of the table and in the Commanding Officer's seat, I looked into the face of my son . . . I get choked up thinking about it now."[38]

The Navy is a success story of how an institution can transform and demonstrate through action its stated values and principles.

MENTORING

Mentoring others contributes to the development of future leaders as well as to building a community-strength team. Leaders are obligated to share the wisdom they have acquired. During my years of service, I spent countless hours mentoring people. It did not matter what their race, background, or gender was. What mattered was that the many people I counseled had access to my thoughts and views about their development. I was fortunate to observe many of my protégés move up to bigger and better opportunities.

ASSIMILATING

From the time I attended integrated high school in 1948 and throughout my career and beyond, I have believed it is important that everyone ***assimilate*** with people from diverse backgrounds and cultures. Learning, empathy, and understanding occur when this is done.

It helps leaders to make the right decisions, to best serve the needs of their people, and to make the organization stronger and more effective. This has been my experience.

YOUTH

Our ***youth*** are the legacy of our efforts as adults. Accordingly, leaders must work in some way to give back to them. Throughout my service and beyond, I have apportioned some time toward the development of young people. Early on, I coached sports teams when my ship was not deployed. I have maintained enduring relationships with the young people in our family as well as their friends, from the time they were very young until now.

At times, when I believed that someone had unfulfilled potential, I tried to establish a relationship to help that person develop. Young people need our support. Leaders must show the way in this area.

[Williams JR]

We live in a world populated by numerous communities. Many believe the community is the strongest social unit beyond the family. As a leader creates teamwork within an organization, building a community—in which people help others—is an approach that yields positive results.

Leaders should encourage their people and their organization as a whole to serve and support communities outside of it. This should include giving back to our youth.

In the Navy, "shipmate" is a term of endearment. Shipmates help their shipmates. This notion of a mariners' community is a part of our heritage and our culture. Throughout the armed forces, similar community cultures exist in which people help others.

DIVERSITY

As a leader works to establish caring and trusting relationships, create teamwork, and build a community, the value of diversity is important.

My father and I noted at the beginning of this chapter that although individual differences may challenge some leaders in achieving unity of effort, we believe that appreciating each person presents the leader with an opportunity to make the organization stronger and improve effectiveness. This is particularly the case when the leader values diversity of backgrounds, experiences, cultures, and thoughts. ***Valuing diversity starts at the top, with the leader.***

The U.S. Navy of today appreciates diversity. This has been reaffirmed continually in the words and actions of the service's leader, the Chief of Naval Operations. Although the Navy is still not where it needs to be in areas such as selecting more minorities and women for officer ranks and enlisted technical skills, the service's commitment and noteworthy progress toward reflecting the face of the nation are beyond question. I have had the privilege to work personally with the Navy's senior leaders on diversity efforts.

The service considers diversity, and its linkage to readiness and operational effectiveness, as a strategic imperative. This is not only because of the changing demographics in our nation, but also

To build a team with the strength of a community, it is essential for leaders to take the time to mentor, both one-on-one and in groups. Leaders have the responsibility to share the wisdom and perspective they have acquired over the years, in an effort to help others develop. (U.S. Navy)

because differences in backgrounds, experiences, cultures, and thoughts make the Navy stronger. And because it is right to value and respect the worth of each individual.

In the 235-year history of the U.S. Navy, today we have the highest percentage of admirals who are minorities and/or women. About 48 percent of the enlisted ranks are minority members (with 52 percent accounting for the majority population). The Chief of Naval Operations has repeatedly stated that today's Navy is the best it has ever been—because of our talented, dedicated people. The Navy is a demonstrative example of an organization and an institution that has continually improved since my father entered it in 1951.

We sometimes receive questions from leaders who ask: "I get it, I value diversity, but what can I do on a daily basis?"

One of the many techniques I have employed regarding this involves ***decision making***. Before meetings that may involve decisions about personnel policies or opportunities, I ask myself, "Who is in the room?"

If my quick scan reveals no women or minorities (other than yours truly), or no diversity of experience (are there enlisted as well as officers?), or no mix of skills (operations, intelligence, supply, and so on), then I correct the lack of appropriate representation. For example, I suggest: "Before we begin the meeting, please ask Master Chief Yvonne Kitchen to attend." In this case, she is the master chief for the staff, and can provide the enlisted perspective. She also happens to be African American.

But ideally, the staff team preplans the who-is-in-the-room situation.

MENTORING

Mentoring is a community activity that helps leaders to develop people.

Mentoring involves people sharing their wisdom, knowledge, and experience with others. It may pertain to those who do not look like each other (woman and man, white and African American, Asian American and Hispanic American, an experienced person in a lower position or status and a lesser-experienced person in a higher one, and so on). Mentoring may also involve people of the same background, experience, culture, or thought.

Leaders should encourage mentoring within their organizations, and should engage in the community activity. They should acknowledge and support established professional ***affinity groups***, chartered to include personal and professional development. I have benefited from affinity groups such as the National Naval Officers Association, the National Society of Black Engineers, and the Black Engineer of the Year Awards (BEYA).

BEYA's Contributions

Dr. Tyrone Taborn, president and chief executive officer of Career Communications Group, is a special person who for more than two decades has hosted the Black Engineer of the Year Awards held annually in Baltimore, Maryland. The awards, mentoring sessions, and employment opportunities at this week-long conference are legendary. Many Fortune 500 companies and all the U.S. armed forces are engaged. BEYA recognizes top students and leaders in private, public, and government organizations. The focus is on science, technology, engineering, and math accomplishments.

In 1995, I was humbled to be recognized. When I could not attend the ceremony due to operational duties, my father accepted

In 2009, Master Chief Williams (Retired, second from left) was honored with a Black Engineer of the Year "Stars and Stripes" award for lifelong contributions in the armed forces. Presenting the award was Vice Admiral Williams (third from left). With them on the podium are Dr. Tyrone Taborn (left) and General Johnnie E. Wilson, U.S. Army (Retired). (Courtesy of the authors)

the award on my behalf. Fourteen years later, in 2009, on behalf of BEYA's Stars and Stripes committee recognizing contributions of those in the armed forces, I was privileged to present a special award to my father for lifelong service. This marked the first time someone who had been enlisted during active-duty service was selected for the Stars and Stripes award. Previous recipients had been generals, admirals, and senior executives. It was a proud moment.

The Centennial Seven

The U.S. Submarine Force was established in 1900. In its first one hundred years, until 2000, seven African Americans commanded submarines. Our group became known as the Centennial Seven.

Since the mid 1990s, the Centennial Seven have conducted mentoring sessions with midshipmen who are interested, as a career possibility, in the Navy Nuclear Propulsion Program and submarines. Our sessions include junior officers who are currently serving. The mentoring has been conducted annually in conjunction with BEYA events. This effort, combined with Navy- and Submarine Force–wide mentoring, is contributing to a positive difference.

Although no one is ready to declare victory in the area of diversity here, there are several success stories. Two of note are those of Rich Bryant and Roger Isom, African Americans who went on to command submarines during the 2000s.

Aside from me, in chronological order the Centennial Seven are:

- *C. A. "Pete" Tzomes*: The first African American to command a U.S. submarine was C. A. "Pete" Tzomes (pronounced Toms). In May 1983, he took command of the USS *Houston* (SSN-713). Tzomes graduated from the Naval Academy in 1967, one of the first thirty African Americans to do so since

The Williams family continues to build a tradition of leadership and service to the country. Serving today are Lieutenant Colonel Ahmed Williamson, U.S. Marine Corps (right, pictured here before his promotion from major) and Captain Dallis Coleman (not pictured), U.S. Air Force, both grandchildren of the master chief. (Courtesy of the authors)

the Academy was founded in 1845. He had a successful tour of duty, was promoted to captain, and retired from duty in 1994. Pete Tzomes serves as a utility manager in the nuclear-engineering field.

- *Tony Watson*: A 1970 Naval Academy graduate, Watson went on to command the USS *Jacksonville* (SSN-699). He later commanded Submarine Squadron One, and then became the first African American submarine officer to be selected as a rear admiral. Now retired, Watson serves as CEO of a consulting firm that specializes in developing corporate strategies and diversity-focused executive searches.
- *Will Bundy*: Enlisting in the Navy in 1964, Bundy rose through the ranks. He served as a chief sonar technician before being commissioned as an officer. In 1988, when he assumed command of the diesel-powered submarine USS *Barbel* (SS-580), Bundy became the first African American to rise from the enlisted ranks to command a submarine. He retired as a commander and earned a doctoral degree. Dr. Bundy now serves as an associate professor at the Naval War College.
- *Joe Peterson*: Before being commissioned as an officer in 1980, Peterson served eight years as an enlisted sailor, an electronics technician. He commanded the diesel-powered submarine USS *Dolphin* (AGSS-555) and was then selected to Navy captain rank. Peterson later retired to serve in private industry.
- *Cecil Haney*: This Naval Academy classmate of mine (1978) assumed command of the USS *Honolulu* (SSN-718) in June 1996. He later commanded Submarine Squadron One. Selected as a rear admiral, he commanded Submarine Group Two Haney also served as the first African American director of Submarine Warfare in the Pentagon. He has been selected to the rank of Vice Admiral

- *Bruce Grooms*: Grooms graduated from the Naval Academy in 1980 and went on to command the USS *Asheville* (SSN-758). He later commanded Submarine Squadron Six, became the first African American commandant of midshipmen at the Naval Academy, and was selected as rear admiral. He commanded Submarine Group Two.

ASSIMILATING

Leaders and followers must be comfortable with people who are different than themselves. This is community behavior. It is important that we ***maintain a global view***. The comfort factor comes from gaining ***understanding*** of people with different backgrounds, experiences, cultures, and thoughts. Leaders should encourage participation in events that observe the ***contributions of different communities***. The history of women, Hispanic Americans, Italian Americans, Asian Pacific Islanders, African Americans, Irish Americans, and Holocaust remembrances are a few examples.

Leaders and followers should endeavor to ***assimilate*** with people who are different. This helps to understand others, and to empathize with them. For example, try experiencing what it is like to be the only male, or the only Caucasian, present in large group activities. For minorities and women, assimilation with society's majority members early in life is helpful.

In my case, assimilation occurred throughout my development, as my father's 1960s–70s submarine-career assignments located our family in communities that were military and predominantly majority-population members. I continue to maintain my African American culture, but learning to assimilate helped me to be comfortable with all people. I believe this made me a better person.

The U.S. Submarine Force was established in 1900. Only seven African Americans commanded submarines through the year 2000: the Centennial Seven. From left in 2009: Pete Tzomes, Tony Watson, Will Bundy, Mel Williams Jr., Joe Peterson, Cecil Haney, and Bruce Grooms. (U.S. Navy)

A GLOBAL FORCE FOR GOOD.

ΦΒΣ

Leaders should reach out to youth, especially in the areas of education, discipline, and character development. As key personnel in a global force for good, Navy leaders should be particularly mindful of finding ways to connect with community and help the young to develop a sense of commitment and responsibility to their society. (U.S. Navy)

On 12 August 2010, Vice Admiral Williams's retirement ceremony was held in Norfolk. Among the attendees was his cousin Operations Specialist Seaman B. J. Wright, who plans to pursue the steps to become an officer. With the admiral here are sideboys Electronics Technician 1st Class (Chief select) Bobbie Branch (foreground) and Operations Specialist 2nd Class Jarvis Stovall (background). (U.S. Navy)

YOUTH

Young people are the legacy of our efforts as adults.

Leaders and their organizations should consider reaching out to give back to our youth, especially in the areas of education, discipline, and character development. Consider this your social responsibility.

The U.S. Navy has many programs that enable sailors to engage with and help young people in local communities. Thousands of senior leaders and junior sailors participate in these programs. Not unlike many others, I have made it a point for many years to apportion time for the young, and for young adults attending colleges and universities. Giving back to the young is truly our legacy of service to others through leadership.

As I accepted command of U.S. Second Fleet on 8 August 2008, among the attendees was Benjamin J. "B. J." Wright, grandson of my father's sister Beatrice Cage. After the change-of-command ceremony, he said he had been so impressed by the pomp and formality, and by the sailors' professionalism. We—his father, a U.S. Army soldier; my father; and I—***took the opportunity*** to describe the opportunities available to young people who choose to serve in today's military.

The following month, B. J. decided to enlist in the Navy as an operations specialist. This is a highly technical job requiring a solid educational foundation, and one for which the service provides superb training and practical experience.

Two years later, in August 2010, Operations Specialist Seaman B. J. Wright was serving in Norfolk, Virginia, at a command that works for Commander, U.S. Second Fleet. As a result of his outstanding performance, his command awarded him the Navy and Marine Corps Achievement medal. It is rare for such a high award to be presented to a seaman who has been in the Navy only two years. B. J. intends to pursue the steps to become an officer.

On 12 August 2010, my retirement ceremony was held in Norfolk. The guest speaker, Admiral John C. Harvey Jr., honored both me and my father. "Master chief," he said, "you served your Navy and your nation with honor and distinction for over twenty-seven years, during a period of time when you loved your Navy far more than your Navy loved you. You never lost the faith that someday, the Navy you loved so much and served so well would take the steps that had to be taken and allow a sailor's talent to be the sole measure of what a sailor can do."[39]

Highlighting my father's efforts during the 1970s, Admiral Harvey noted, "You unlocked the doors, you took the first steps, and you helped put us on the right path." Mel Sr. received a standing ovation.

B. J. was in attendance to witness all the naval fanfare and emotion. During my speech, I tried to honor those who paved the way before me while also pointing toward the work of the future and those who follow me—including, in our family, Operations Specialist Seaman B. J. Wright.

As Albert Einstein said, "Only a life lived for others is a life worthwhile."[40]

SUMMARY

- This book is intended to be another resource for those of any age who are interested in leadership or serve as leaders, or who would like to gain insight into the story of a father-son master chief and vice admiral.
- Navigating is the art and science of knowing one's location while moving safely and in a timely manner to a destination.
- *Navigating the Seven Seas* proposes a nautical theme representing the maritime domain of the U.S. Navy.
- The experiences of a master chief and a vice admiral show how we navigated to a destination of increased leadership responsibilities through our Seven Cs: character, competence, courage, commitment, caring, communicating, and community.
- This book addresses several implied questions regarding who a leader is, what a leader does, and why and how a leader performs.
- Although the context of experiences is in Navy, the Seven Leadership Cs are relevant to all fields, regardless of the reader's

occupation or leadership situation, whether military or civilian, public or private industry—and regardless of the reader's background, culture, and gender.

Leadership is the *art* and *science* of achieving desired effectiveness by making decisions, developing people, creating teamwork, serving needs, and inspiring action to realize the leader's vision.

Leadership can be learned, and the Seven Cs offer a helpful method for thinking about ways to do so.

- **character**

  This most important Leadership C is essential to the end, ways, and means of ***realizing the leader's vision.*** The formulation of the leader's vision, the team's understanding of it, the commitment to take right and timely action repeatedly toward realizing the vision are central to leadership.

- **competence**

  Leadership involves having competence in ***achieving desired effectiveness*** (results, performance, or outcomes), as defined by the leader. A leader must be competent as he or she guides the organization.

- **courage**

  Leadership necessitates courage in ***making decisions.*** Leaders should consider the facts, opinions of a diverse group, instincts and intuition, and be decisive at the right time.

- **commitment**

  A commitment to ***developing people*** is essential. This includes providing opportunity for them to realize their full potential. The leader must be capable of trusting others, which means accepting risks associated with delegating authority, and permitting some mistakes by those gaining experience.

- **caring**

  Leadership includes caring, or ***serving needs***. Individual people, money, and time are all required to accomplish an objective, and the team as a whole has different requirements. The leader must remain aware of all of these and work diligently to obtain needed resources, while also having consideration of people's needs.

- **communicating**

  Inspiring action is accomplished through communicating. People want to be inspired by the leader. However, an inspirational speech without a plan and the right and timely action may be labor lost. The leader must develop forward-looking plans with the team, and take action while creating a sense of urgency. Leaders must assess progress, adjust, adapt, and execute.

- **community**

  Leadership involves regard for community when ***creating teamwork***. With better-prepared and developed individuals, the leader works to create a cohesive team, so that the whole is greater than the sum of the individuals.

A large organization such as the U.S. Navy can make institutional and cultural changes that transform and demonstrate its values and principles. *Navigating the Seven Seas* shows how the Navy accomplished this.

The contemporary world faces major challenges—and leaders must transform these into opportunities. Accordingly, the art and science of leadership must be studied, learned, practiced, and refined by as many individuals as possible. This will help to achieve desired effectiveness and realize a better world.

Following active-duty service, we have continued to practice the tenets set out in this book. I, Master Chief Mel Williams Sr. (Retired), went on to serve for many years as the leader of food service at the Soldiers and Airmen's Home in Washington, D.C., for a total of fifty years in government service. Today, Ruth and I continue to provide love and advice to family members and other young people.

In 2010, I, Vice Admiral Mel Williams Jr., decided to transition from the Navy after thirty-two years of commissioned officer service (with an additional year of enlisted service accrued at the Naval Academy Preparatory School). Demonstrating confidence in my leadership abilities, the Chief of Naval Operations nominated me for assignment as commander of the U.S. Strategic Command, a four-star position. However, this joint-service combatant command was assigned to a U.S. Air Force officer.

Therefore, I gratefully rejoined my family in the D.C. area to seek opportunities within our community—a continuation, as it has been for Mel Sr., of serving and leading others. Father and son both truly believe in the importance of the Leadership Seven Cs, which helped us to navigate while serving as leaders in the U.S. Navy and beyond, in civilian life.

NOTES

1. Eleanor Roosevelt, quoted in John Cook, ed., *The Book of Positive Quotations* (Minneapolis: Fairview Press, 1997), 166.
2. Letters to author from parents, August 1973. Author's personal collection.
3. United States Naval Academy, Mission, http://www.usna.edu///homepage.php.
4. Norman Vincent Peale, quoted in John C. Maxwell, *The Power of Attitude* (Tulsa, Okla.: River Oak Publishing, 2001), 132.
5. Anonymous, quoted in Fred A. Manske Jr., *Secrets of Effective Leadership* (Columbia, Tenn.: Leadership Education and Development, Inc., 1999), 234.
6. Robert Greenleaf, *Servant Leadership* (New York/Mahwah, N.J.: Paulist Press, 1977), 27.
7. Henry David Thoreau, quoted in Cook, ed., *The Book of Positive Quotations*, 272.
8. Melvin G. Williams, SD1 (SS), "Independence Day Every Day," *The Snorkel* (USS *Thomas Jefferson*), vol. 3, edition 4, p. 4.
9. Chester A. Wright, *Black Men and Blue Water* (Bloomington, Ind.: AuthorHouse, 2009), 318.
10. B. C. Forbes, quoted in Cook, ed., *The Book of Positive Quotations*, 461.
11. J. F. Kennedy, quoted Cook, ed., *The Book of Positive Quotations*, 400.

12. Glenn Knoblock, *Black Submariners in the United States Navy, 1940–1975* (Jefferson, N.C.: McFarland, 2005), 181.
13. Ibid., 250.
14. Letter from Admiral E. R. Zumwalt Jr. to Senior Chief Petty Officer Williams, 14 June 1974. Author's personal collection.
15. Memo from David H. Bagley to Superintendent, U.S. Naval Academy, 4 January 1975. OP-O1P:BJP:klr, Ser: 915-74. Department of the Navy, Office of the Chief of Naval Operations, Washington, DC.
16. Memo from MSCM Melvin G. Williams to RADM W. R. Dowd Jr., Commander, Naval Supply System Command and Chief of the Supply Corps, 25 August 1976. Author's personal collection.
17. Memo from James W. Nance, Assistant Vice Chief of Naval Operations," to Rear Admiral W. R. Dowd Jr., 3 Sept. 1976. "Second endorsement on MSCM M. G. Williams, USN ltr of 25 Aug 1976." Department of the Navy, Office of the Chief of Naval Operations, Washington, DC. Copy in author's personal collection.
18. Letter from LTJG S. F. St. Thomas to RADM W. R. Dowd Jr., 12 March 1976. Navy Department, Naval Supply Systems Command, code OP 4 (MCPOF). Copy in author's personal collection.
19. Dr. Martin Luther King Jr., quoted in Alex Ayres, ed., *The Wisdom of Martin Luther King, Jr.* (College Park, Md.: Meridian Books, 1993), 35.
20. Ralph Waldo Emerson, quoted in Cook, ed., *The Book of Positive Quotations*, 405.
21. Thomas Paine, quoted in Robert A. Fitton, ed., *Leadership Quotations from the World's Greatest Motivators* (Boulder, Colo.: Westview Press, 1997), 211.
22. Aristotle, quoted in *Thoughts on Leadership: The Forbes Leadership Library* (Chicago: Triumph Books, 1995), 55.
23. Manske, *Secrets of Effective Leadership*, 57.
24. Albert Schweitzer, quoted in Maxwell, *The Power of Attitude*, 149.
25. Booker T. Washington, quoted in Fitton, ed., *Leadership Quotations from the World's Greatest Motivators*, 249.
26. Will Rogers, quoted in Cook, ed., *The Book of Positive Quotations*, 423.
27. Navy Unit Commendation, Secretary of the Navy John Lehman

to USS *Jack* (SSN-605), for service 7 June –16 July 1981. Copy in author's personal collection.

28. Meritorious Unit Commendation, Secretary of the Navy James H. Webb Jr. to USS *Woodrow Wilson* (SSBN-624), for service 1 January 1985–28 January 1987. Copy in author's personal collection.
29. Congratulations, CNO Washington to USS *Louisville*, March 1991. Copy in author's personal collection.
30. Meritorious Unit Commendation, Chief of Naval Operations Admiral J. L. Johnson to USS *Nebraska* (SSBN-739), for service 18 August 1994–1 January 1997. Copy in author's personal collection.
31. Meritorious Unit Commendation, Chief of Naval Operations Admiral V. E. Clark to Carrier Group Five Commands and Staffs, for service 1 January–31 December 2001. Copy in author's personal collection.
32. Marcus Annaeus Seneca, quoted in Cook, ed., *The Book of Positive Quotations*, 80.
33. Franklin Delano Roosevelt, quoted in Cook, ed., *The Book of Positive Quotations*, 121.
34. Lao-tzu, quoted in Cook, ed., *The Book of Positive Quotations*, 80.
35. Abraham Lincoln, quoted in Donald T. Phillips, *Lincoln on Leadership: Executive Strategies for Tough Times* (New York: Warner Books, 1992), 145.
36. Anonymous, quoted in Cook, ed., *The Book of Positive Quotations*, 287.
37. Martin Luther King, quoted in Ayres, ed., *The Wisdom of Martin Luther King, Jr.*, 48.
38. Knoblock, *Black Submariners in the United States Navy, 1940–1975*, 256.
39. Admiral John C. Harvey Jr., quoted in Meredith Kruse, "New Commander Takes Helm at Second Fleet," *Virginian-Pilot*, 13 August 2010, http://hamptonroads.com/2010/08/new-commander-takes-helm-second-fleet.
40. Albert Einstein, quoted in Cook, ed., *The Book of Positive Quotations*, 86.

INDEX

Acara, Bernard, 4
Acara, Nettie, 4
accountability, xiv, 52, 59, 64–66
Afghanistan, 93–94, 95, 96, 98, 99
African American Anthem, 7
African American community: equal opportunity in, 13; jobs for African Americans, 6; skin color issues, 4
African American service members: aboard submarines, 88–89; assignments as stewards, 8, 133–34; conditions for, 56; equal opportunity changes, 53–59, 69–70; father and son, unique service of, xi–xii; mentoring by senior petty officers, 8, 10; minority and women service members, 57, 150; stewards, recognition of, 41, 60–63, 120–21; as vice admirals, 94
Air Force, U.S., xix–xx
Arctic region, 99
Aristotle, 72
Arlington Cemetery, 63
Armel, Lyle, 35, 38–39, 40
Army, U.S., xix–xx
Asheville, 156
assimilating, xv, 140, 146, 156
attitude, positive, xiv, 2–3, 8, 10, 12–13, 26–27
authority, delegation of, xvi

Bagley, David H., 56
Bainbridge, 99
Barbel, 155
Bataan, 135
Black Engineer of the Year Awards (BEYA), 151–53
Black Men and Blue Water (Wright), 41
Black Submariners in the United States 1940–1975 (Knoblock), 54, 145

Branch, Bobbie, 160
Bridges, Ruby, 74
Bryant, Rich, 153
Bundy, Will, 155, 157

Cage, Beatrice, 161
caring: faith, xv, 102, 103, 107–8; family, xv, 102, 103–4, 108–11; importance of, xvii, 101–2, 105–6, 165; leader, xv; people, xv, 102, 104–5, 111–14; self, xv, 102, 106–7
Carl Vinson, xix
Carp, 75, 76, 81
Centennial Seven, 153, 155–56, 157
Chafee, John, 35
character: commitment and character development, 22, 25; determination, xiv, 2, 12–13, 21, 26; honesty, 12, 26; humility, xiv, 3, 13, 14, 27; importance of, xv–xvi, 1–2, 164; integrity, xiv, 2, 12, 18, 21, 25, 26; positive attitude, xiv, 2–3, 8, 10, 12–13, 26–27; Rickover Effect, 21–22, 25; servant leadership, xiv, 3, 13, 28
Coast Guard, U.S., xix–xx
Cohen, George A., 41
Cold War, 79, 81, 87–89
Coleman, Dallis, xii, 12, 154
Comfort, xix
command ombudsmen, 131
commitment: character development and, 22, 25; as core value, 3, 73; to developing people, xvi, 71; excellence, xiv, 25, 72, 75, 84–86; goals, xiv, 72–73, 77, 86–87; importance of, 71–72, 165; of leaders, 83–84; service, xiv, 72, 73–75, 83–84, 165; teamwork, xiv, 73, 77, 79, 81, 87–100, 165
communicating: barriers to, 130–31; communication skills, improvement of, xii, 127; extemporaneous speaking, 129–30; importance of, xvii, 117–18, 165; inspiring, xv, xvii, 117, 118, 131–34, 165; listening, xv, 118–19, 127–28, 131; strategic context of messages, 129; transmitting, xv, 118, 119, 127, 128–29; understanding, achieving, xv, 118, 119, 128–29
community: assimilating, xv, 140, 146, 156; diversity, xv, 140, 141–45, 147, 150; importance of, 139–40, 146–47, 165; mentoring, xv, xvi, 140, 145, 151–56; regard for, xvii; youth, xv, 140, 146, 158–59, 161–62
competence: importance of, xvi, 29–30, 42, 164; improvement, continual, xiv, 30–31, 40–41, 47–48, 50; judgment, xiv, 30, 40–41, 47; performance, xiv, 30, 38–40, 45, 164; preparedness, 43; progress, xiv, xvii, 30, 31–38, 42
Constellation, 144
courage: accountability, xiv, 52, 59, 64–66; as core value, 3, 52; decisiveness, xiv, 52, 66–69, 164; definition of, 52–53; equal opportunity changes and leadership courage, 53–59;

importance of, xvi, 51, 164; initiative, xiv, 52, 69–70; selflessness, xiv, 52, 70, 162
Cummings, Elijah, 121

Danzig, Richard, 60–61
decisions: courage to make, xvi; decisiveness, xiv, 52, 66–69, 164; factors in decision making, 67
Desert Storm, Operation, 89–90
determination, xiv, 2, 12–13, 21, 26
Dilworth, Sally, 4
Dilworth, West, 4
disaster response missions, 94, 96–98
discipline about ships, 119
discrimination, xii, 121, 141–45
diversity, xv, 140, 141–45, 147–50
Dixie, 75
Dolphin, 155
drug use and addiction issues, 35, 38, 39

education: emphasis on and importance of, 7, 33; integration of schools in New Orleans, 74; racially integrated education, 8, 14; segregation in, 14, 74
effectiveness of leaders, xvi, 25, 29–30, 42
Einstein, Albert, 162
Emerson, Ralph Waldo, 69
Enduring Freedom, Operation, 93–94
Enterprise, 60
"Eternal Father" ("Navy Hymn"), 114–15
excellence, xiv, 25, 72, 75, 84–86
extemporaneous speaking, 129–30

faith, xv, 103, 107–8
family, xv, 13–14, 103–4, 108–11
Flag Day experience, 129–30
food service aboard ships, 39–40
Forbes, B. C., 43
Fowler, Jeffrey L., 124
Freedom, 99
friends, 111
Fulton, 75

goals, xiv, 72–73, 77, 86–87
Golden Rule, 106, 107
Gravely, Alma, 136
Greenleaf, Robert, 28
Grooms, Bruce, 156, 157
Groton, Connecticut, 14

Haiti relief effort, xviii–xx, 98
Hancock, 75, 78, 79
Haney, Cecil, 155, 157
Harmon, Leonard, 134
Hartman, Dick, 88
Harvey, John C., Jr., xviii, 162
Hassayampa, 144
Hendrickson, Bill, 92
historical markers, 62, 63, 121, 122, 124, 133–34
Hoephner, K. T., 88–89
Hollister, 75, 79
Holloway, James L., III, 11, 23, 35, 57
homeland defense missions, 94, 96–97, 98
honesty, 12, 26
Honolulu, 155

honor, 3–4, 18, 21
Houston, 153
humility, xiv, 3, 13, 14, 27
Hyman, Henry, 11

Ignatius, Paul, 35
improvement, continual, xiv, 30–31, 40–41, 47–48, 50
initiative, xiv, 52, 69–70
innovation, 90
inspiring, xv, xvii, 117, 118, 131–34, 165
integrity, xiv, 2, 12, 18, 21, 25, 26
Iraq, 12, 89–90, 96, 98, 99
Isom, Roger, 153
Iwo Jima, 135

Jack, 87–88
Jacksonville, 155
James K. Polk, 35, 75, 81
Johnson, Lyndon, 35
judgment, xiv, 30, 40–41, 47
July 4th article, 32

Kennedy, John F., 51, 114
King, Martin Luther, Jr., 64, 139
Kitchen, Yvonne, 150
Kitty Hawk, 144
Kitty Hawk strike group, 93–94, 95, 145
Knoblock, Glenn, 54, 145
Korean War, 79
Kunzman, Douglas, 136

leadership: art and science of, xiv, xv, xx, 164; character of leaders, 57–58; commitment of leaders, 83–84; effectiveness of leaders, xvi, 25, 29–30, 42; examples set by leaders, 25; follow-up actions, 128; Haiti relief effort and, xviii–xx; learning skills for, xiv, xv; Navy culture and, xiii–xiv; Seven Cs of, xiii, xiv–xx, 163–66; vision and, xv–xvi, 1, 26, 129, 164
Lehman, John, 88
Lincoln, Abraham, 117
listening, xv, 118–19, 127–28, 131
Louisville, 89–90, 91

Mannings, Harriet, 4
Mannings, Horace, 4
Mannings, Ida Dilworth, 4
Mannings, Lushus, 4
Marine Corps, U.S.: core values of, 3, 52; Haiti relief effort, xviii–xx; war-fighting competency, 99
maritime strategy, 94, 96–100
McCorkle, Gary, 111
meetings, diversity in, 150
mentoring, xv, xvi, 8, 10, 140, 145, 151–56
Mesa Development, 11
mess management specialist (MS) rating, 55, 56, 59, 121, 123, 125–26
Messman's Chronicles, The (Miller), 121
Middendorf, J. William, II, 35
Miller, Doris, 134
Miller, Richard, 121
mistakes, 2
Moore, Pearl, 10
Moorer, Thomas, 35
Mullin, James, 119

National Naval Officers Association, 151

National Society of Black Engineers, 151
Native Americans, 6
Nautilus, 22
Naval Academy, U.S.: education of Mel Jr. at, 10, 16–21, 42, 166; historical marker at, 63, 121, 122, 124; mission of, 18
Naval Academy Preparatory School (NAPS), 16–18, 21, 166
Navy, U.S.: advancement opportunities in, 12–13, 31–38; boot camp experience, 8; change in, institutional and cultural, xiii, 166; command ombudsmen, 131; core values of, 3, 52, 73; discipline about ships, 119; discrimination in, xii, 121, 141–45; drug use and addiction issues, 35, 38, 39; equal opportunity in, 11, 53–59, 69–70, 120–21, 142–45, 147, 150; food service aboard ships, 39–40; Haiti relief effort, xviii–xx; married service members, 109, 111; mess management specialist (MS) rating, 55, 56, 59, 121, 123, 125–26; minority and women service members, 57, 150; opportunities in, xiii–xiv; racial attitudes and issues in, 38–39, 144; segregation in, 8, 10; stewards, recognition of, 41, 60–63, 120–21; stewards in, 8, 41
"Navy Hymn" ("Eternal Father"), 114–15
Navy Mess Attendant School, 62, 63, 121, 133–34
Nebraska, 35, 46, 49, 90, 92–93, 145
Nelson, Eric, 112, 113
New Mexico, 6, 10–11
Nixon, Richard, 35
Norman, Flora, 8, 10
Norman, Lawrence, 8, 10
North Carolina, 63, 121
nuclear-powered submarines, development of, 22

Okinawa, 12, 143
opportunity, 43–45

Paine, Thomas, 71–72
Patton, George S., 77, 130
Peale, Norman Vincent, 27
Penn, B. J., 136
Penn, Loretta, 136
Pentagon career, 11, 16, 23, 35, 41, 53, 82, 142–44
people: caring about, xv, 102, 104–5, 111–14; developing potential of, xvi; development of, 165; fallibility of, 64–65; friends, 111; individual worth of, xiii, 140; preparedness, responsibility for, 43
performance, xiv, 30, 38–40, 45, 164
Peterson, Joe, 155, 157
Petters, Mike, 136
Pettes, Ella Graves, 6, 13
Pettes, Robert A., 6, 10–11, 13
Phillips, Richard, 99
Piedmont, 23, 35, 38–40, 59, 118–19
Pinckney, William, 60–61, 121, 134

piracy and counter-piracy training, 99
plan of action, development of, xvii
positive attitude, xiv, 2–3, 8, 10, 12–13, 26–27
Prairie, 75, 141–42
preparedness, 43
Priest, Charles, 11, 37
progress, xiv, xvii, 30, 31–38, 42

Quarreles, Maurice, 7

racial attitudes and issues: challenge of in Navy, 38–39, 144; discrimination, xii, 121, 141–45; equal opportunity changes, 11, 53–59, 69–70, 120–21, 142–45, 147, 150; in South Africa, 141–42
Rawls, Forest, Jr., 23
Reason, Diane, 136
Reason, Paul, 136
relationships, 27
responsibility, 25
Rickover, Hyman G., 21–22, 25
Rickover Effect, 21–22, 25
Rockwell, Norman, 74
Roosevelt, Eleanor, 2
Roosevelt, Franklin, 114
Royal Navy, 114

St. Louis, Missouri, 5–6
St. Thomas, S. F., 58
Samuel Gravely, 136
Schweitzer, Albert, 83
Second Fleet, U.S., 94, 96–100, 135
self, xv, 106–7
selflessness, xiv, 52, 70, 162
Seneca, Marcus Annaeus, 101
sense of humor, 3
Sequoia, 35, 59
servant leadership, xiv, 3, 13, 28
service, xiv, 72, 73–75, 83–84, 165
Seven Cs of leadership, xiii, xiv–xx, 163–66. *See also* caring; character; commitment; communicating; community; competence; courage
Seven Seas, xiii
shipmates, 147
smiling, 3
Soldiers and Airmen's Home, 166
South Africa, 141–42
stewards: African Americans as, 8, 133–34; recognition of, 41, 60–63, 120–21, 122, 124, 133–34; school for, 63
Stewart, Frank, 89–90
Stovall, Jarvis, 160
Strategic Command, U.S., 166
submarines: African American service members aboard, 88–89; Centennial Seven, 153, 155–56, 157; costume dinner aboard, 81; courage and responsibility for mistakes, 65–66; crew organization on, 90, 92; decisiveness and mistakes made on, 68; Mel Jr.'s submarine force service, 22, 25, 42, 153, 157; Mel Sr.'s service aboard, 75; nuclear-powered, development of, 22; strategic deterrence mission, 90, 92–93; submarine force, establishment of, 153, 157

Taborn, Tyrone, 138, 151, 152
Tacoma, Washington, 7–8, 10
teamwork, xiv, xvii, 73, 77, 79, 81, 87–100, 165
Thomas Jefferson, 11, 31–32, 34, 36, 37, 75, 81
Thoreau, Henry David, 29
time-management strategies, 106–7
transmitting, xv, 118, 119, 127, 128–29
trust, 26
Tzomes, C. A. "Pete," 153, 155, 157

understanding, achieving, xv, 118, 119, 128–29
U.S. Black Engineer Information Technology, 138
Units K-West and B-East U.S. Navy Mess Attendants Association, 60–63

Vietnam War, 79
vision, xv–xvi, 1, 26, 129, 164
visualizations, 129

Warner, John W., 11, 35, 82
Washington, Booker T., 84
Washington, D.C., 14–15, 166
Watson, Tony, 155, 157
William Pinckney, 60–61, 63
Williams, Dimple Manning, 4, 13
Williams, Donna Ree, 14, 109, 110, 121
Williams, Dora Ruth Pettes, 6, 12, 13, 23, 33, 103–4, 108–9, 121, 166
Williams, John, 4
Williams, Kenneth, 7, 14, 74, 103
Williams, Melvin G., III, 109, 110
Williams, Melvin G., Jr.: achievements of, recognition of, 138; appearance of, xiv; assimilation of, 156; Black Engineer of the Year Award, 151–53; caring, importance of, 105–6; Centennial Seven member, 153, 157; change-of-command ceremony, 11, 35, 161; character of, xiv; command opportunities, 21, 25, 44; commissioning of, 35; communication style of, 127–30; courage and leadership, 63–70; diversity, value of, 147, 150; education of, 14–15, 44; excellence, commitment to, 84–86; faith of, 107–8; family background of, 7, 13–14; family of, 23, 33, 103, 108–11; Florida Flag Day experience, 129–30; at football game, 20; goals of, 86–87, 104; Haiti relief effort, xviii–xx; historical marker dedication, 121, 124; influence of on Mel Sr., 11–12; initiative of, 69; *Jack*, service on, 87–88; *Kitty Hawk* strike group, service on, 93–94, 95, 145; *Louisville*, service on, 89–90, 91; military service of, 11, 83–84; natural ability of, 42; Naval Academy education of, 10, 16–21, 42, 166; Navy, transition from, 166; *Nebraska*, service on, 38, 46, 49, 90, 92–93, 145; oath

of office, administration of, 24; office activities, 112–14; pipe habit, unlighted, 67–69, 137; professional milestones achieved by, xii, 44–45; progress and advancement, 42–50; promotion ceremony for nephew, xii–xiii; retirement of, 160, 162; *Samuel Gravely* christening ceremony, 136; Second Fleet, commander of, 94, 96–100, 135; self, sense of, 106; service and rank of, xi–xii; submarine force service, 22, 25, 42, 153, 157; teamwork examples, 87–100; time-management strategies, 106–7; *Woodrow Wilson*, service on, 87–89; work experience of, 15

Williams, Melvin G., Sr.: achievements of, recognition of, 41, 54, 57–58; appearance of, xiv; assimilation, importance of, 146; athletic abilities of, 31; Black Engineer of the Year Award, 151–53; *Carp*, service on, 75, 76, 81; character of, xiv, 10–12, 57–58; courage and equal opportunity changes, 53–59, 69–70, 142–45; *Dixie*, service on, 75; education of, 7–8, 10, 33; examples set by, 108; excellence, commitment to, 75; faith of, 103; family background of, 4–7; family of, 33, 103–4; at football game, 20; *Fulton*, service on, 75; goals of, 77; Good Conduct Medal, awarding of, 75; *Hancock*, service on, 75, 78, 79; historical marker dedication, 121, 124; *Hollister*, service on, 75, 79; *James K. Polk*, service on, 35, 75, 81; keynote address given by, 120–21; mentoring opportunities, 145; military service of, 8–10, 12–13, 73–75; *Nebraska*, in control room on, 49; newspaper editorial responsibility, 32, 34, 35; oath of office, administration of, 24; Pentagon career of, 11, 16, 23, 35, 41, 53, 82, 142–44; *Piedmont*, service on, 35, 38–40, 59, 118–19; pipe habit, unlighted, 137; *Prairie*, service on, 75, 141–42; professional milestones achieved by, xii; progress and advancement, 31–38; retirement activities of, 12; retirement of, 10; self, sense of, 102; *Sequoia*, service on, 35, 59; service and rank of, xi–xii; Soldiers and Airmen's Home, service at, 166; teamwork examples, 77, 79, 81; *Thomas Jefferson*, service on, 11, 31–32, 34, 36, 37, 75, 81; young people, support for by, 146

Williams, Robert, 4, 13

Williams, Sarah, 4

Williams, Sharon, xiii, 7, 11, 14, 23, 33, 103, 121

Williams, Trinity Marie, 109, 110

Williams, Veronica, 7, 12, 14, 23, 33, 103, 121

Williamson, Ahmed, xii–xiii, 11–12, 154

Williamson, Mattrice, xiii
Wilson, Johnnie E., 152
Winfrey, Oprah, 12
Woodrow Wilson, 87–89
Wright, Benjamin J. "B. J.," 160, 161–62
Wright, Chester A., 41

youth, xv, 140, 146, 158–59, 161–62

Zumwalt, Elmo, Jr.: courage of, 53; legacy of, 11; Mel Sr.'s service to at Pentagon, 35, 53; reform policies of, 11, 53, 54, 55, 80, 144

ABOUT THE AUTHORS

Master Chief Mel Williams Sr., U.S. Navy (Retired), a submarine-qualified enlisted sailor, entered the Navy during the Korean War in 1951 and went on to serve twenty-seven years, retiring in 1978. His assignments included tours in an aircraft carrier, surface ships, submarines, the presidential yacht *Sequoia* (with Presidents Lyndon B. Johnson and Richard M. Nixon), and the Pentagon, where from 1970 to 1977 he served as leader of the Secretary of the Navy and Chief of Naval Operations Dining Facility. During this period, Master Chief Williams provided enlisted leadership advice to senior Navy leaders and initiated efforts to help ensure equal opportunity for all people serving in the Navy. His final Navy assignment was as command master chief on board the USS *Piedmont* (AD-17).

Master Chief Williams's awards include the Meritorious Service Medal, Presidential Unit Commendation, Good Conduct Medal (six awards), National Defense Service Medal (two awards), Korean Defense Service Medal, Submarine Silver Dolphins, and Fleet Ballistic Missile Submarine Patrol pin, with nine stars. He and his wife live in the Washington, D.C., area.

Vice Admiral Mel Williams Jr., U.S. Navy (Retired), a nuclear-trained submariner, served in the Navy for thirty-two years as a commissioned officer and one year as an enlisted sailor. His operational assignments included commanding the U.S. Second Fleet, Submarine Group 9, and Submarine Squadron 4; and serving as commanding officer of the USS *Nebraska* (SSBN-739, Gold crew). Other key assignments included deputy commander of U.S. Fleet Forces; director of Global Operations, U.S. Strategic Command; chief of staff, *Kitty Hawk* Carrier Strike Group, during initial combat in Operation Enduring Freedom following attacks on 11 September 2001; and executive officer on the USS *Louisville* (SSN-724) during Operation Desert Storm's initial combat in 1991.

A 1978 graduate of the U.S. Naval Academy, Vice Admiral Williams holds a master's of science in engineering and attended Harvard's JFK School of Government. His military awards include Distinguished Service Medal (two awards), Defense Superior Service Medal, Legion of Merit (five awards), Defense Meritorious Service Medal, Meritorious Service Medal, Navy and Marine Corps Commendation Medal (five awards), and the Navy and Marine Corps Achievement Medal (two awards). Civic recognitions include Black Engineer of the Year Awards for Professional Achievement, National Society of Black Engineers Golden Torch Award for Lifetime Achievement in Government, and the Thurgood Marshall Award for Service and Leadership. He lives with his wife and family in the Washington, D.C., area, not far from the Williams Senior home.

The **Naval Institute Press** is the book-publishing arm of the U.S. Naval Institute, a private, nonprofit, membership society for sea service professionals and others who share an interest in naval and maritime affairs. Established in 1873 at the U.S. Naval Academy in Annapolis, Maryland, where its offices remain today, the Naval Institute has members worldwide.

Members of the Naval Institute support the education programs of the society and receive the influential monthly magazine *Proceedings* or the colorful bimonthly magazine *Naval History* and discounts on fine nautical prints and on ship and aircraft photos. They also have access to the transcripts of the Institute's Oral History Program and get discounted admission to any of the Institute-sponsored seminars offered around the country.

The Naval Institute's book-publishing program, begun in 1898 with basic guides to naval practices, has broadened its scope to include books of more general interest. Now the Naval Institute Press publishes about seventy titles each year, ranging from how to books on boating and navigation to battle histories, biographies, ship and aircraft guides, and novels. Institute members receive significant discounts on the more than eight hundred Press books in print.

Full-time students are eligible for special half-price membership rates. Life memberships are also available.

For a free catalog describing Naval Institute Press books currently available, and for further information about joining the U.S. Naval Institute, please write to:

Member Services
U.S. NAVAL INSTITUTE
291 Wood Road
Annapolis, MD 21402-5034
Telephone: (800) 233-8764
Fax: (410) 571-1703
Web address: www.usni.org